20 PRINCIPLES OF
PRODUCTIVITY

Alex Genadinik

ISBN-10: 1543236987

ISBN-13: 978-1543236989

DEDICATION

Dedicated to my mother and grandmother who are the biggest entrepreneurs I know.

CONTENT

FOREWORD

The advice in this book is based on research, personal experimentation with productivity techniques, and the experiences of 1,000+ of my clients.

My hope is that this collection of vetted productivity strategies will help you do better in everything you do today and for the rest of your life.

I wish you the best of luck in your business, and hope that the ideas in this book can contribute to your success. Enjoy the book.

BEFORE WE START

A VERY WARM WELCOME TO YOU

I want to start by wishing you a very warm welcome. I am excited to have you aboard. I wrote this book from my heart, knowing that if you use the strategies in this book, you will significantly improve many facets of your life. After coaching over 1,000 entrepreneurs, I understand that people who succeed in business and in life are the ones who keep learning and striving to make themselves better as entrepreneurs and professionals.

In this book I share quite a bit about my own productivity journey, challenges, and even bloopers. While you will get to know quite a bit about me, I hope to someday get to know you. My door is always welcome to my readers. I'd love to hear your thoughts on the book, and how you think it can be improved.

My personal email address is alex.genadinik@gmail.com and I look forward to hearing from you after you complete the book.

GIFTS FOR YOU AT THE END OF THE BOOK

There are 3 additional free resources for you at the end of the book. They include additional free training, mobile apps to help you start a business, and a way to get personalized advice from me. There is nothing more helpful than getting personalized advice for your unique situation. Read about all the ways in which I help you at the end of book.

THE STRUCTURE OF THIS BOOK

<u>Part I</u> is about making you more productive in your immediate work right now, today, this week and this month.

<u>Part II</u> is about long-term, big picture productivity, and a deeper look into who you are and what it means for you to be productive in your life.

LIST OF ALL THE ASPECTS OF PRODUCTIVITY YOU WILL LEARN ABOUT IN THIS BOOK

1) Productivity fundamentals

2) Focus

3) Self-discipline

4) Building healthy work habits

5) Productivity apps and software

6) Minimizing distractions

7) Organization

8) Outsourcing

9) Delegation

10) Business process optimization

11) Coaching and masterminds

12) Planning projects ahead

13) Overall health maintenance for productivity

14) Improving your memory and cognitive ability

15) Time management

16) Prioritization

17) Scheduling

18) Self-awareness to make wiser choices

19) Goal-setting

20) Reversing procrastination

21) Boosting motivation

22) Productive market testing for products and business ideas

23) Meeting productivity

I added a couple of bonus aspects of productivity. My hope is to add even more aspects of productivity in the future revisions of this book.

PART I:

IMMEDIATE PRODUCTIVITY BOOST

CHAPTER 1:
INTRODUCTION TO PRODUCTIVITY

"The way to get started is to quit talking, and begin doing."

- Walt Disney

Congratulations on starting the book. Did you know that more than half of the people who buy books never start reading them? Not starting is obviously the single worst productivity fail. So you are already ahead!

1. What you are going to get in this book and who the book is for

The ideal reader of this book is a business owner, entrepreneur or a professional hoping to become more effective at what they do, and boost their career. This book is also great for students because if you make yourself more productive earlier in your life, that extra boost in productivity will remain with you throughout your school and career, and help you become more successful at everything you decide to work on for the rest of your life.

If your business is just you or only a handful of employees, this book should be ideal for you.

Most entrepreneurs don't fail because of business reasons. Business strategy is often easy to fix or correct. What's difficult to fix is the actual entrepreneur. The more an entrepreneur can accomplish, the more he gives his business a chance to succeed. Conversely, entrepreneurs with inefficiencies tend to accomplish less, which decreases their chances of success.

In my practice, the productivity and the level of professional approach is pound for pound one of the biggest indicators of whether the entrepreneur will succeed.

It is easy to fix and adjust parts of business strategy, but it takes years of work to change a person.

Productivity can also be a confusing term that means different things to different people. Does it mean an app that will magically help you get more done? Does it refer to business processes like delegation, outsourcing, automation, or optimizing some of the ways you work to make you more efficient? Or does productivity refer to getting enough motivation to finally end procrastination and begin working on some project? Or does it mean the productivity of your entire business?

In this book, I compiled a very complete list of productivity strategies that touch on everything from the minute to minute productivity techniques that make you more productive in the moment, to much bigger and deeper life questions that will help to direct your life's work in the direction it was meant to by helping you discover your life's true purpose. Pursuing your life's true purpose will give you boundless motivation to help you overcome procrastination and propel you forward throughout your life.

I was inspired to write this book in this all-inclusive way because I was frustrated by the broad and frankly confusing word "productivity" which had baffled me in the early part of my education and career.

Once I got a firm grip on all the elements of productivity, I began to accomplish more, and find success in my work.

But I don't want to mislead you. There are parts of productivity that I still struggle to conquer. I, like you, am allowed to be human. As we move through this book, I'll share some personal case studies and anecdotes where you and I will have a chuckle at my own little failures.

The goal of these case studies is to make the book full of practical examples in addition to theory. The book also contains many exercises that are designed to help you begin your journey into various aspects of productivity.

Although the subject matter of this book is serious, much of the tone of this book is joking or teasing because I wanted for you to have fun reading (a productivity tip in its own right), and for me to have fun writing. I apologize in advance if you don't find me quite the comedian I imagine myself to be.

Lastly, let me give you the lens through which to see my advice, and maybe give you a sense of entrepreneur frustrations

I was trying to solve.

Not to brag, but who are we kidding? Pardon me as I brag a little. In addition to being an entrepreneur myself, I've personally coached over 1,000 entrepreneurs in various capacities, and my work has helped millions of additional entrepreneurs throughout the world, of every age, education level, social background, talent, and temperament. These interactions gave me an incredible sense of the entrepreneurial journey.

Do you know what similarities I noticed among all those entrepreneurs?

The biggest commonality is that almost every single one of them fails.

Yes, I just admitted that outright and without hesitation. You may be wondering why they fail if I am supposedly so great. Shouldn't I be able to wave my magic wand and make them succeed? I don't do their work for them. I only advise them. It is up to them to do the work to succeed, which they almost unanimously don't implement well.

This brings me to the second thing entrepreneurs have in common - hard work. Many first-time entrepreneurs swear by how much and how hard they will work, but they are almost unanimously united by terrible work ethic and a less than professional approach to the work.

Did I just say that? I think so. It's only Chapter One - a bit early for you to think that I am a complete jerk so let me explain that in a more palatable way. What I meant to say is entrepreneurs get excited, daydream about their success, work themselves up with excitement, talk to their friends to get positive reinforcement, and on the wings of that excitement finally either sit down to work or to write a business plan, they immediately encounter challenges.

And oh my, the challenges are suddenly not exciting. In fact, they are frustrating. Sad face goes here. If I wasn't such a literary coward, I'd put three sad faces one by one, but I don't know if I can take the heat from the grammar nazis who will proclaim me a simpleton of expression. Anyhow, let's continue. After a few frustrating attempts to resolve the newly discovered business challenges, the entrepreneurs whom I coach, help, and whose success I worry about as a mother would, begin the failure process.

Sometimes the failure process is simply the decrease and gradual cessation of work on the business. But don't worry, I still give those entrepreneurs a medal for participation because I'm a mensch, which is coincidentally something that you should consider in my favor if you decide to leave me a review on Amazon or Kindle! Wink wink.

Productivity tip 1:

It may be obvious that I was having fun writing this book. And that is a productivity tip in itself. It would be utter boredom and drudgery to write such a book in a serious and businesslike tone. I would not have enjoyed doing that, would have put it off, and would have been more likely to quit writing at some point along the way. Instead, I was having fun writing, which means I was looking forward to my writing sessions. This helped me finish the book faster and have a better time writing it. As long as you don't feel like hitting me over the head with a stick in retaliation for all the bad humor, we can call this a productivity success.

I also want to share a small secret with you. I've always had a dream of being a creative writer. You may already be smirking that I write how-to books instead of more creative genres because maybe I am not creative enough for those.

I admit, truly creative works require more talent and creative risk. The style in which this book is written, however, where I sprinkle humor throughout the book, is allowing me to practice a few creative elements, which is something I had always wished I did more of. And that partial fulfillment of a long-term dream made writing this book even more fun, enjoyable and productive.

When possible, don't be afraid to take a few more liberties in your work if they allow you to do things you are interested in. It will keep your interest and motivation levels higher, and that will result in you doing more work with better results.

2. Start yesterday

Had I watched less TV and made myself a better student while I was doing my middle school and high school homework, I might have gotten better grades, gotten into a better university, graduated while retaining more skills and information, and used those skills and information to write a better book for you.

Instead, you get this. While I believe this is already a good book, everything can always be better, including this book. You can achieve more and better things during your career if you boost your productivity earlier rather than later. Improving yourself has a snowball effect that accelerates as you go. The sooner you start, the further you will end up.

Even though this book is generally for entrepreneurs, business owners and professionals, if you are a middle school, high school or a college student, and you make use of the strategies in this book earlier in your life rather than later, it can help you achieve more throughout your life.

If you are an entrepreneur, I can share from experience that in the early stages of starting my business, there was so much stress to simply not fail that it created a mad scramble and desperation to break even financially. There didn't seem to be mental room or time to focus on acquiring productivity skills. I needed to make money, not learn how to neatly organize my desk or play around with productivity apps.

Before my business became financially viable, I couldn't be bothered with learning skills that seemed at the time to be non-essential. Luckily for me, I stumbled into a few of the tips in this book by simply having a sense for what was working better. Nearly all the mistakes I made early on can be attributed precisely to my NOT following the productivity strategies in this book. Let me share just a few of my early mistakes:

Mistake 1: I did not seek advice from a coach or a mastermind group and ended up making all the mistakes on my own. A 10-minute conversation with an expert can sometimes help to prevent you from making very large business mistakes, and save you months of time and quite a few Shekels.

So don't be a putz. Learn from my mistakes and save your Shekels. Finding expert help today is easier than ever. Simply join Facebook and LinkedIn groups around your area of interest and post questions there. Many people in such groups are industry experts who love helping others in their community.

Mistake 2: I gave in to the financial stress that comes with starting a business. While feeling the financial stress, I began focusing only on making a short-term dollar (Shekel?). What do you think happens when you sacrifice the long-term vision for short-term success? You end up pursuing mediocre business strategies, which end up costing you months of backtracking, losing more Shekels over the long-term, and potentially even more un-earned Shekels due to not reaching your potential.

Mistake 3: I also didn't try to improve the quality of my focus while I worked. I allowed my brain to get distracted by new email and Facebook alerts informing me of the latest dumb things people were doing. And honestly, I still have not completely recovered. I am a bit of an online addict. If I can be honest, strengthening my focus over a long period of time while working has been a very challenging process for me. FYI, if you aren't already doing so, this is where you go "aww" as you feel a little bit bad for me.

The takeaway is that there are always good reasons to put off productivity improvement. The ironic thing is that if you do focus on improving your productivity earlier rather than later, it will help you do everything you are currently doing better and faster. In hindsight, one of the things I would improve about my own journey as an entrepreneur would be making myself much more productive sooner rather than later.

3. Personal story and experience from your author

As mentioned earlier, I was a complete productivity dope in high school and early college. I had a sense that I could be more productive, but I didn't know how to achieve that. I used to just "wing it" with my school work and that didn't help me get good results. It could be that since you got this book that you are just "winging it" when you do your work and you are looking for more structure and guidance on how to improve your process. If that is true, this book will really help you.

My first productivity breakthrough came during early college. I was working part-time as a security guard to help pay my bills - clean uniform (at least in the beginning), white shirt, flashlight, a fake clip-on tie and all. How official of me, I know. Why am I telling you this? Because I treated the 8 hours of my security guard duty as a creativity exercise in how I could most painlessly waste the time until I got to go home. Early on in my security guard career I realized that I should be using at least some of my guard time to do college work, which considering my rebellious spirit, largely meant not actual class assignments, but working on things I was curious about.

I was getting lost in all my creative ideas and the tasks that I had to do. Out of necessity and part accident, I started practicing my first successful productivity strategy and created my first to-do list. I saved it on a USB memory stick. Do you remember using those? If you do, congratulations, you are probably old like me. "Happy together in misery" face goes here.

I immediately loved putting tasks on my to-do list and crossing them off when they were completed. I carried that USB everywhere, and to my own surprise, I ended up maintaining that simple text-based to-do file for years through college and during my early work career. I still maintain a to-do list on most days. I just use different technology.

Maintaining a to-do list was one of the things to which I attribute my success. I'll touch on all the benefits of to-do lists later in the book, but here is a summary of how they can help you.

1) It can help you break big daunting tasks into smaller manageable ones
2) It can help you start on tasks and build momentum in projects
3) 3) It can help you add more positive emotions to your work by building on small successes
4) Every morning you will wake up with a plan of action, knowing exactly what to do that day, so not waste time meandering

5) It can help you get in touch with your nerdy and organized self, which isn't a productivity tip in itself, but boy did getting in touch with my nerdy self help me embrace necessary skills for success

Some people attribute coolness to entrepreneurship, But let's be honest here, if you aren't partially a nerd, can you really be a successful entrepreneur? Think about it.

What's my point here? Start using to-do lists. If you are not already using to-do lists, they will help you in an amazing way. And if you are already doing this, NERD!

4. Which Productivity?

Productivity is a very overused term. Each of the following very different aspects of productivity are considered aspects of productivity.

1) Procrastinating and never sitting down to do anything
2) Sitting down to work, getting distracted, and not working
3) Sitting down and working poorly
4) Making you more resourceful at overcoming challenges and roadblocks
5) Getting the right kind of help
6) Working on the right things
7) Team productivity
8) Full business productivity

Productivity is one of those terms for which everyone seems to have their own definition. I wrote this book with the intention to bring all the disparate subfields of productivity under one umbrella. I'll cover these and many additional aspects of productivity later in this book.

I will help you reduce procrastination and strengthen your focus to get you working as effectively as possible for longer periods of time. I'll also help you choose tasks to work on, and explain how to choose tasks which will be more likely to get you closer to your goals. I'll also help you understand how to tell which life goals are specifically ideal for you.

5. Helpful practice to start the book: journal your distractions

You might have thought that you would get off easy until at least chapter 2, but here is your first exercise. Get a piece of paper or create a digital file if you are into the environment like I am, and use it to write down your distractions during every hour of work for an entire day.

A distraction can be any alert, phone call, or a co-worker that interrupts you while you are working. You may be surprised how many distractions occur during the day. For many people, they happen so frequently that they become very difficult to even track.

You can also keep track of things that not only distract you, but put you on a completely different work track. These don't just interrupt you. They are much worse because they divert you from your chosen path. These types of instructions include emails that get you to do anything non-essential, unplanned calls, impromptu meetings that aren't about your main focus that day, and anything else that diverts time and attention from the tasks on which you are supposed to be giving your focus.

If I think back to my college days, these two kinds of distractions made up almost the entirety of my college experience. When I was supposedly "working" on my school work, my attention was constantly pulled away from it by friends, phone calls, emails, socializing with study partners, or the old classic of doing homework while watching TV.

I've mostly gotten control over my interruptions, but I still have times where I feel bad saying no to people, or when I give into my own weaknesses and check the latest alerts on my phone and email. It is a work in progress for all of us, so don't be ashamed to find out how much of your day's work is ruined by distractions.

The point of this exercise is to find and identify things that waste your time. Once you identify the sources of your distractions, you can focus on working to reverse those behaviors.

6. Second helpful practice to start the book: examine your past 30 days of work: did they get you closer to your goals?

In the previous section, we took a look at your daily distractions. But what if you are a perfect worker who doesn't suffer from being distracted, but instead works on the wrong tasks?

Wouldn't all your time worked be 100% unproductive if you are working on the wrong tasks?

To identify some incorrectly chosen or ineffective tasks, look back at your last 30 days of work, and identify which tasks actually brought you closer to your goals. If you are old and have a bad memory like I do, instead of trying to recall what you worked on, just keep track of things you work on for the next 30 days (thought you were off the hook for not remembering? Not so fast!).

The goal of this exercise is to help you identify your most productive, goal-oriented tasks to help you understand the types of tasks to work on, and which tasks to avoid moving forward. As much as we think that we know what our most productive tasks are, there can be many surprises if you take the time to look it over and evaluate your work.

7. Weird and honest case study

This book is full of researched theory and exercises for you to practice that theory. But do you know what it can't possibly have? It can't have advice based on what you and your unique situation require. To address your unique situation, you will need to not only use the tools I'll arm you with in this book, but also experiment with how you apply them, and calibrate your experiments to make the tactics ideal for your unique situation.

To illustrate this point, let me give you an example of how I discovered what makes me most productive.

Everyone has a different aspect of the productivity puzzle where they excel, and where they could use some improvement. For example, I have no problem being motivated or with procrastination. My problem is getting distracted or getting bored while I work. When I work, it sometimes feels as though my brain is looking for more stimulation, and I run into the problem of surfing the web or checking email and losing focus on my immediate work.

In fact, later in this book, you and I will do a challenge for this together. Well, I already did the challenge since by the time you get the book I will have finished writing it. But I hope that you won't leave me hanging and that you will do the challenge too.

After I tried many techniques to improve my focus during work, do you know what worked best in the end? You will never guess. What worked in the end, broke all or most productivity rules.

What worked for me was buying a big bag of sunflower seeds and munching on them for hours. I am able to maintain good focus during those hours because munching on the seeds gives me that extra bit of stimulation I need to not feel bored. I am able to sit there and keep working on my task. And if I have a bottle of diet coke (even worse!) to go with the seeds, that makes me even more productive.

If I was going off theory alone, I would never guess that this would be what keeps me focused. In fact, later in this book I explain why eating at your desk is really bad. Plus, the constant act of picking up seeds is itself distracting. But it solves another productivity issue by keeping me sitting at the computer, and not getting distracted by other things. The seeds turned out to be a smaller distraction that solved a bigger distraction, and made me more productive. I only discovered that by experimenting. If I simply followed theoretical advice, I would never have stumbled upon this little solution. So please experiment with how you implement the strategies in this book, and find what works for your unique situation.

Don't just passively read this book. Practice the techniques in this book by applying them in the real world. Try different combinations of productivity techniques. The more you try things and work on them, the more productive you will make yourself. Over time, you will get closer and closer to finding what's ideal for you. But you will never get there with just theory.

Since so much of your productivity journey is unique to you, your habits and mindset, you are welcome to send me questions about your challenges to my personal email. I'll be happy to do my best to offer extra advice. That is an option open to all readers of this book. You can read more about how to contact me at the end of the book where I explain all the extra gifts available to my readers.

CHAPTER 2:
PRODUCTIVITY FUNDAMENTALS

Congratulations, you survived Chapter One! Considering that about half of the people who buy books never read them, and that many others quit early on, you are probably in the 75th percentile of all people who bought this book. Now that you have momentum, you are very likely to finish the entire book, and get as much out of it as possible. Go you!

Since I can't give you a physical ribbon for making good progress through the book, if you do finish this book, just for being so good, towards the end of this book I'll give you a very cool and kind of secret productivity tip on how I wrote this book quickly and efficiently. I just won't tell you exactly where it is in the book so that you won't cheat and skip ahead to it. You will have to read the whole book to find it.

In this chapter we will explore core productivity fundamentals that will serve as a foundation for each chapter moving forward.

1. Singular focus within a task

Your ability to focus intensely and for a prolonged period of time is one of the biggest keys to productivity. The longer and more intensely you can focus on a single task, the more productive you will immediately become.

Throughout this book, I'll be giving you tips and exercises to boost your focus. Even if you choose to work on an entirely wrong task which might result in a 100% wasted effort, the productivity gods will still be envious of your ability to focus (while also kind of laughing at you for working on the wrong tasks).

Let me explain this idea of focus a bit further. You might think that all focus is the same. After all, if you are focusing on a task, then you are focusing on a task! Duh.

If we examine the idea of focus by looking at it through a microscope, we can notice that we might experience entirely different levels of focus throughout a day or even while working on the same task at different times.

Imagine you are writing a school paper or a book like I am doing right now. Let's already assume that you are not watching TV and that you are not going to be distracted by your phone or social media. Even without productivity killers like TV, your phone, or social media, your focus while working can be affected in these very different ways:

- You could be unmotivated and dragging in your writing, waiting for quitting time

- You could be motivated but tired which would make it difficult to focus

- You could be writing during a part of the day where you

are less productive

- You could be writing during a part of the day where you are more productive

- You could be writing with confidence

- You could be writing without confidence

- You could be hungry

- You could be well-caffeinated, well-fed, and raring to go

- You might have distracting thoughts pertaining to personal or professional problems

- You might not have such distractions

- You might simply hate writing, and maybe you can't wait for it to be over

- You may or may not be experiencing physical or emotional pain or discomfort

- And many more physical and emotional variables that will have a direct impact on the quality of your focus.

- Any combination of the above

Or

- You might be writing in an absolute state of flow, or "the zone" where you are well-caffeinated, laser focused, not sleepy, not tired, not hungry, not thirsty, happy, confident and extremely motivated by the belief that what you are working will bring you closer to your goals by leaps and bounds. This is the ideal state of mind with which to work. If you achieve this, you will accomplish much more and higher quality work.

In all of these emotional and physical states, you are focusing on a task. But in all of them, the quality of your focus and with it, the quantity and quality of the end product will be profoundly different.

A part of this has to do with you being sufficiently self-aware, to be able to get yourself to an ideal state of focus, and your ability to maintain your focus. Even a state of flow or "the zone" doesn't last forever, and your energy can wane.

2. Identify highest value tasks: exercise and eventual discipline

We all have moments where we seem to be really busy, doing a lot of work, yet not making any major progress in our overall project. Squirrels refer to this as spinning their wheels, but not all humans have figured out how to recognize it when it is happening to them.

Sadly, you are a human and not a squirrel. Us humans spin our wheels without actually moving forward when we make poor decisions about which tasks and projects will get us closer to our goals, and which will have minimal or no impact.

As a student or working professional, you must work on honing your judgement regarding which tasks will get you closer to your goals, and which won't. Be mindful of it.

For business owners, there is an 80-20 rule where in many cases 20% of our work results in 80% of our progress, and the other 80% of our work only gets us 20% closer to our goals.

This rule typically applies to things that are already on our project plan or to-do list. But there are probably ALWAYS tasks or ideas we have not thought of that might be better than anything we already have in your line of vision.

If you work with a good business coach or belong to a mastermind group, these can be sources of bigger and better ideas that can transform your task list to contain only the most effective tasks that will propel your business forward. Additionally, if you make a poor choice of what task to pursue, a coach or a mastermind group can help to point out your mistake, and save you from losing time and money.

If you don't focus on choosing the right tasks, all kinds of fodder might creep into your to-do list, and squirrels will put you to shame when it comes to moving your life and projects forward. But if you identify your top 20% tasks, get the right coaching and advice, and do a few simple things to help your mind reach extra levels of clarity and creativity, you can absolutely beat a squirrel, and even many humans. We'll cover how to do all of this in future chapters of this book.

If you don't use any other techniques in this book other than ones that help you boost focus in your daily work and in how you choose projects to work on, you will still do wonders for your productivity. I know this first hand because improving my focus in these two areas did wonders for my own productivity. After I improved how I chose projects, choosing only the top 20%, and after I improved my focus when I was sitting down to do the actual work, I began to produce better results, and my business grew while I was able to work less since I got rid of 80% of my unnecessary time-killing tasks.

Getting rid of 80% of my low-return tasks, freed up enough of my time to give me mental space to think about bigger picture projects for my business. It also gave me time to look for coaching and mastermind groups I could join which in turn gave me access to intelligent peers and experts who were able to suggest even better ideas for my business.

3. Delegation

Delegation is a process by which you hand off the tasks on your company's overall to-do list to someone else.

Do people ever call you lazy? If so, congratulations! This is where your laziness will finally be an advantage.

Even if you are not lazy, you probably understand that you can't do or know everything on your own, and the more tasks you can hand off to someone else, the more of your time you will free up to complete additional important tasks.

If you are a student trying to delegate your homework, nice try. This section is not for you. Do your own homework!

If you are running a business, you can find many different types of people you can hire to delegate tasks:

- Freelancers online

- Day laborers or local concierges who will perform physical work on-site

- Temp workers

- Contractors

- Employees

- Co-founders

- Family members (if you ask nicely)

- Other companies you partner with if you negotiate your partnership details well

If you are just starting a business, freelancers, temp workers, day laborers and local concierges are the cheapest option because you don't need to sign any contracts with them, and most of them don't require office space. All you have to do is hire them online.

Hiring college students for free or very cheaply might seem like an good option, but most college students are not fully professional just yet, and many of them can be either flaky, or simply require too much training. For every brilliant college student, you will find five flakes (sorry college students who are reading this), and it might end up cheaper and more efficient for you to just do the work yourself. Plus, the candidate search and interview process you will need to go through before you find a good college intern will be a tremendous time drain.

Another problem with hiring people is that they like to be

paid in real Shekels, and not monopoly money or promises of stock options which, let's face it, will never materialize.

We can commiserate about not having money to afford delegation of enough tasks to be truly lazy, but let's take a look at some inexpensive tasks that you can begin delegating early.

Outsourcing is a large part of delegation. Outsourcing online has become very affordable. You can hire freelancers to perform many business tasks like the ones listed below:

- Anything time consuming and repetitive which you can write instructions for, and have anyone else simply follow those instructions

- Design services

- Engineering services

- Video recording, especially spokesperson and talking head videos that are popular to create YouTube ads

- Technical skills you don't have

- Social media posts and updates

- Text, audio or video editing

- Transcription services

- Crappy blog posts since most freelancers don't know enough about your business to write great blog posts, but are able to create cheap and mediocre ones

Here are a couple of examples of a tasks that I would consider to be in a gray area where it is your call whether to outsource or not:

1) Writing quality blog posts
2) Outsourcing SEO services

Writing quality blog posts: I am going to go out on a limb and assume that you want your articles to be of high-quality. In the age of the Internet that's a lot to ask, I know. What does it take for an article to be of the highest quality? It requires author expertise in the subject matter, a deep level of insight, and good writing.

Most content and article writers you can hire as freelancers will write with good grammar, but they are often not experts in your industry. Most of their research prior to writing an article amounts to looking up similar existing articles online and either taking many ideas from those articles or rewording large parts of what's already written.

The gap in the necessary article quality and what outsourced content writers can deliver is too great for me to see them as a service that a company that is serious about their content should hire on a regular basis. Hiring freelance article writers is okay for very basic articles. Although I'd challenge that strategy by asking why you'd need to write very basic articles in the first place, since your readers can already find plenty of that elsewhere online. I'd suggest writing insightful and high-quality content instead of regurgitated material.

Outsourcing SEO services: this is probably the most classic way in which small business owners get screwed. There is an entire industry of below subpar SEO service companies. Yes, I said "below subpar" because subpar is still somewhere within reason. These companies are far worse than that. These "below subpar" SEO companies sell and provide services that they know won't materialize into traffic or clients for you. The only thing they know is that there are many small business owners who don't want to learn or do SEO (it really isn't rocket science, and I encourage you to give it a try), and want to hire someone to do it for them cheaply.

These below subpar SEO companies are often located in countries where even a very cheap US salary is good money, and are happy to get small business clients that can't pay much by first-world standards.

It is a perfect match of a lazy business owner with opportunists who just want to siphon off a bit of cash before the lazy business owner realizes that their SEO services aren't working.

Don't get me wrong, there are plenty of high-quality SEO service providers. But unless you work for a wealthy company, you won't be able to afford them to the extent that they need to be hired to have a significant positive impact for your business.

For my business, I preferred to learn and do my own SEO. This has done wonders for my business, and I recommend that you do SEO in-house. Just learn it and do it. It is actually quite simple for the most part. Keep in mind, one of the free gifts offered to readers of this book at the end of it is a choice of a free online course. You are welcome to choose an SEO course to help you get started with it on your own, and save you money by not having to outsource it.

If you are working as a manager for a slightly bigger company and you have employees, delegation is an absolute part of your job. If this is your situation, you must learn delegation techniques in a much more extensive way than this book can cover. What I'll say is that you must do your best to match the most important tasks to the people who would do them best not only in the short term but also in the long term, which means that you need to get to know your employees enough to know what types of tasks move and inspire them. If you can tap into your employees' natural curiosity that will motivate (good luck with that if they are millennials) and inspire them long-term, and will help to naturally make them better at the tasks they are given.

4. Automation

Automation is another good topic for the lazy. If there is a business process that happens repeatedly, see if it can be automated with a software tool. If it can be automated, that might free up a lot of your time which you can use to work on higher-level tasks which will be more productive in moving your business closer to its goals.

If you have a budget for automation, you can also outsource a few development hours to online freelancers who can make specific tools that will help your business processes move more smoothly.

If you have ideas for custom software that can be built to

automate something in your business, you can find quality and affordable software developers to hire on UpWork.com.

Here are some examples of software tools:

i. HootSuite - automation social media update

ii. ConvertKit - email automation

iii. InfusionSoft - sales process automation

iv. Evernote - management of many small tasks in one place

v. WordPress plugins - there is a very large variety of WordPress plugins for automating and improving just about everything related to your website.

These are just some examples of tools that can help you automate a few common business processes. If you have other business processes that are unique to your business which take up a lot of your time on a regular basis, be sure to search for possible tools to automate it instead of doing repetitive tasks over and over.

5. Budget for delegation and automation

Budget...Shekels...ugh...paying sucks, I know. Even if you want to outsource and delegate, you might simply not have enough money to be able to afford hiring anyone. Here are four ways to come up with the money so that you can start hiring.

1) Raising money - I created a popular and free YouTube video with 15 unique ways to raise money for your business. Some of them are standard, and some are pretty "out

there," but if you are truly ready to work hard and make your business succeed, you should be ready to try even the things that seem a bit "out there." Here is the link to that video:

https://www.youtube.com/watch?v=KGVgamPNPNY

2) Make extra income online - if after watching the video on 15 ways to raise money, you didn't find a strategy that would work for you, you can try to supplement your income by making money online. Here is my popular free YouTube video with 40 ways to make money online:

https://www.youtube.com/watch?v=-jstQysWmfQ

Note on the videos: they were made a few years ago so please excuse the production quality which isn't at a professional level. But the advice in the videos is still relevant.

3) Start by hiring small - you can hire small by spending just $100 or less a month for tasks that can free up your time to focus on higher priority tasks. For $100 you should be able to get at least 10 hours of a freelancer's time, and that 10 hours can result in a significant productivity boost. If you think about it, $100 is nothing in the grand scheme of things. Even if you are a student, it is a fine amount to invest in your business each month. If your business grows or you see significant help from this initial outsourcing, you can begin to incrementally increase your spending.

4) Grow revenue and profit of your business - this is my favorite strategy because it is the most sustainable strategy

long-term. When I was first starting my business, it wasn't making much money. Even $100 seemed to me like a bigger risk than it actually was because it was putting my business even further in the red. The accumulation of all the stress and pressure weighed on my mental state and made me tighten my budget as much as possible.

There was the already difficult reality of my finances and there was an even more severe sense of pressure and uncertainty that comes with owning a small business which is struggling. Unfortunately for me, I succumbed to the latter.

And yes, I know that I am a hypocrite for telling you not to give in to that pressure and to try to keep cool, calm and collected as much as possible while I myself didn't. I'll just assume that you will be mentally stronger than I was.

I was only able to allocate a budget for hiring after my business turned a profit. If you don't have a strong stomach for losing money, waiting until you have enough revenue or profit might be a good strategy for you as well.

In general, the more you can spend, the bigger chance you will give your business to grow faster. The less you can spend, the more you will have to rely only on the hard work and hustle of the founding team, which in many cases is just you.

Let's say that you will wait until you turn a profit before you can outsource. If you are running a small business, revenue can often be unpredictable. Depending on the type of business, revenue can fluctuate up to a few hundred percent from month to month and quarter to quarter. Larger companies tend to budget things for the year or quarter ahead, but if you are just starting your business, I would recommend budgeting only a month in advance.

When you start hiring, hire slowly until you find great freelancers or contractors, and boost your budget as you see fit moving forward. If you are risk-averse, building up slowly will allow you to avoid making big mistakes.

6. In the business vs. on the business

This section covers one of my favorite productivity strategies for long-term success. But it might sound a little confusing. After all, how do you work "on" the business? Do you sit on top of it? If it's an online business, you can't even sit on anything!

When you work in your business, you are doing things that the business requires like building your product, hiring, promoting, dealing with finances, or any other task needed by the business to keep operating. This is standard and does not need to be explained.

A contrast to all these tasks is "working on your business." When you work on your business, you are working on improving the skills you use when you working in the business.

An example of this is improving your marketing skills so that next time you do marketing, you will do it better and achieve better results from your efforts.

Let's do another example. When you build your product, you are working in your business. But when you are working on improving your hiring skills, outsourcing skills, or product building skills, you are working on your business because those tasks will help you create better products moving forward.

Let me be VERY serious here: the quality of everything you do will be one of the biggest overall determining factors in whether your business succeeds or fails. Let me illustrate this with a few examples.

Example 1: You and your competitor can make a YouTube video to promote your individual businesses. You might get 3 views (probably all of them from your grandmother showing it to her grandma friends and telling them how smart you are), and your competitor might get 1,000,000 views. Why would this happen? Simple, your competitor probably made a higher quality video and promoted it more effectively. Even though the same video marketing strategy was used, the quality of execution was the difference between success or failure. One outcome was a result of good execution, and the other outcome was the result from insufficient level of execution (your grandmother will probably come after me for saying that about you).

Example 2: When I wrote my first book, app, YouTube video, or online course, none of them succeeded overnight. Each of them succeeded only after I learned how to improve my skills at producing and promoting them. Customers began to truly benefit from my products and my products began to grow and succeed financially only after I got all these products to a high enough degree of quality.

I had to work on my business to improve my skills and make myself better at what I do. Once I improved to a certain level, my business grew. The opportunity for improvement is infinite. My motto is "everything can always be done better" so try to spend at least 10-20% of your work time on your business, improving your skills and business processes. Long term, it will be one of the most productive things you can do because even small and incremental improvements will add up to tremendous gains over the course of many years.

One thing I always regret is not being able to make something better sooner. When I work on anything today, one of the things I focus on most is product quality. Even after I release products, I work on improving them on an ongoing basis. In fact, currently, I am working more on improving my existing products, books, and courses rather than creating new ones.

If you have an online presence to your business, quality will be even a bigger potential dealbreaker. If you have an online product like a book on Amazon, YouTube video, or a listing of your service on Yelp.com, if your customers like your product, you will get a boost from good reviews. If your customers are not impressed with your product, you will get a decrease in customers due to the inevitable bad reviews. Online, quality is the biggest difference-maker between success and failure.

7. Working in chunks or bursts

We already talked about the importance of focus. Unfortunately, people have a limit on how long they can focus on one task, and how much total focus they can maintain throughout a day.

Besides making yourself better at choosing the things on which you focus, I want to focus (meta!) on how to structure your focus during your work.

There is a very famous technique to maximize focus. It is called "The Pomodoro Technique." The Pomodoro Technique works by scheduling an intense burst of focus followed by a short break to give your mind a break, and repeating that cycle over and over throughout the day.

The Pomodoro technique suggests certain time intervals. We'll get to that later, but you can start with any of the following:

- 10 minutes of intense focus with a 5-minute break if you are just starting

- 20 minutes of intense focus with a 5-minute break as you begin to feel more comfortable doing this technique

- 30 minutes of intense focus and a 10-minute break as you practice this technique and become better at maintaining your focus for a longer period of time

- 45 minutes of intense focus and a 15-minute break as you keep getting better

- 1 hour of intense focus with a 20-minute break as you keep improving

- As you become very good with this technique, you can

work up to 90 minute work intervals with 30-minute breaks

The intensity of your focus when you sit down to do your work will help you make tremendous progress in your work, and the breaks will help your mind refresh. Some of the most ideal breaks are ones where you can do some stretching or go for a walk outside, preferably in a park if you have one nearby. It is also nice to have a healthy snack on your break. Just don't keep sitting at your work area during your break.

People call these periods of intense focus chunks, bursts or sprints. Whatever. The idea is the same: break your work into intense bursts.

You can take this idea to another level by treating entire projects this way. For example, you might take full days or even weeks during which you intensely focus on a specific project. Devoting so much focus to just one project without being distracted by other tasks will help you make tremendous progress in that project. Later in this book, I'll explain how I used this tactic to write 14 books in 56 days, which is quite a productivity triumph.

8. Can you run your business working 1 hour per day using productivity strategies?

What's up, my contingent of lazy readers? Your ears perked up, didn't they? Just for that, my recipe for you is to work twice as much. Everybody else, listen up. While I don't recommend that you only work one hour per day since you could accomplish so much more if you worked eight equally productive hours instead of one, I'll explain how you could pull off working just one hour a day using the principles we discussed in this chapter. On a serious note, if you have a full-time 9-5 job, this will be ideal for you. While you will be able to spend less hours working, you may have some money to spend on outsourcing and delegation.

Since you only have one hour, you can't do any actual work yourself. All you can do is use that time to delegate tasks, hire people to outsource and automate processes, answer emails, and take important (hopefully sales) meetings or calls.

One hour of work per day gives you time to:

- Communicate and write instructions for your employees and freelancers

- Automate and outsource your marketing. Promotion tasks that can be automated are: SEO, YouTube marketing, marketplace marketing where you sell on marketplaces like Amazon, Etsy, Udemy or many other marketplaces because some of those marketplaces do some of the promotion for you, and advertising by buying ads on Google Adwords, Facebook ads or any other ads.

- Take calls and answer emails

If you delegate your work to employees and freelancers and automate your marketing, you can successfully run your business on just one hour per day. Granted, you would bring more muscle to every task required by your business if you worked 8 or more hours. If you are a motivated entrepreneur, 12-16 hours per day is not unheard of. Are you up for a 16-

hour workday challenge? Your business would likely be better off if you put more work into it. But it is very possible to run a business on just one hour per day if you master many of the productivity principles covered in this chapter.

CHAPTER 3:
HOW TO IMPROVE YOUR FOCUS

1. Practical exercise: starting the Pomodoro Technique

I already mentioned the Pomodoro Technique which is a strategy to help you achieve optimal focus. With this technique, you choose a duration for a short burst of intense focus followed by a break, the duration of which you choose. The official Pomodoro Technique recommends a certain time for focus and breaks, but since you know yourself best, as you start this, you choose the amount of time during which you feel you can sustain a strong focus, and a break that you feel will be sufficient.

Just don't reverse the Pomodoro Technique and pick five minutes of work and break for the next two weeks.

Here is a reasonable way to ease into implementing this technique in your work. Plan ahead for one of your next work days to have a large block of uninterrupted time during which you can begin applying this technique. A large block of time can be two to six hours. By giving yourself a long period of time during which you focus on one project, you will be able to relax and not stress about time pressure. Plus, you will be able to get through a few Pomodoro cycles within a few hours.

I know what you just did. You probably put my suggestion in the back of your mind and already dismissed it by thinking you will do it later.

I know you did that! Let's try again. Really, think about your schedule for this and next week, and block out some time to practice these strategies because what's the point of knowing them, but not actually taking the steps to make yourself the productive rock star that I want you to be? You only become more productive once you practice these productivity tactics, and become better at implementing them correctly and effectively over time.

2. Discipline yourself

Does the title of this section make you slightly worried? Yes? Good! I'm about to become a crossbreed of a gangster and a doting mother, telling you to get your act together.

I am joking because I wanted to have a third chance in a row to urge you to get off your butt (tuchas - look this word up on Google. It's a classic) and discipline yourself to take the necessary steps to begin practicing the strategies in this book, starting with the Pomodoro Technique.

Before working productively becomes a habit, you should do your best to discipline yourself to work more and work better. The truth is that your productivity and success starts and ends with you. If you aren't up for the challenge, no magical strategies or techniques will have a chance of working.

One thing you MUST take seriously is that your success begins and ends with your actions.

The kind of results you get is going to directly correlate with the effort you put into improving your productivity. If you ever find yourself scratching your head, wondering why some things aren't working out as you had hoped, first and foremost look inside yourself and your own actions. Did you do the best you could? Did you get the right help in terms of education (good job getting this book and actually reading it), or coaching? And did you take the steps to apply what you had learned? Did you try to apply what you learned again and again until you got it right, and tried to identify what caused things to go wrong?

An overwhelming majority of people do not do the things I just mentioned. That's why I am harping on this point, suggesting that you take the time and devote a necessary amount of mental energy to begin practicing and applying the strategies. If you don't, you will get only minimal benefits from this book.

Let me share a real-life example about a client I used to coach. During our coaching calls, he was engaged and receptive to my suggestions. But when I gave him tasks to work on between our calls, he never did them. Most people don't. Most people don't even get to their most important tasks, so this is actually somewhat normal albeit surprising at first glance.

If this happens, I start to challenge clients on their time management, motivation, self-discipline, and stated business priorities. As I dug into how this client was managing his time, I realized he had no discipline. This client was giving into every possible distraction. If his friends invited him to a bar to watch sports, he would join them and drop his work. If people needed his help, he would be open to providing it. If there was a fun show on TV, he would watch it instead of working on his business. While it is great to be social, open and gregarious, he had no discipline and ended up constantly putting off his responsibilities.

Don't be like my client. Take the bull by the horns. Make your work and your success one of your top priorities. Your friends won't do that for you. Only you can do that for yourself. If you put the responsibility of your own discipline and eventual success squarely on your shoulders, it will help you say no to frivolous distractions, and devote more time to focus on your dreams.

3. Work is boring and even worse, frustrating. I quit!

What happens when you begin to focus on actual work that gets you closer to your goals?

You realize that the actual work truly sucks. It does so unapologetically and most mundanely. The actual work is often tedious, confusing, frustrating, fraught with failure which is the byproduct of your trial and error, filled with self-doubt, and lonely in its existential struggle against the nothingness that you are able to show for your work, which is all you have before you succeed.

Naturally, you should quit. If there was ever an ideal point for quitting, it is the moment you have to wake up from your sweet daydreams, and begin to do real work. I am not even joking. Up to now, you've gotten a tremendous amount of enjoyment from your business or life goals by letting yourself indulge in hope, sweet daydreams, extra endorphins, and excited yet pointless brainstorming with random newbies who puff out their chest exaggerating their business experience.

But actual work brings none of that. It brings negative things like confusion, frustration, low confidence, etc.

Quitting might seriously be the most emotionally intelligent thing you can now do.

But you won't quit, will you?

Statistics show that while you might think to yourself that you are not a quitter, most people do quit at exactly this point in achieving their dreams.

Knowing all this, make damn sure YOU don't quit! Success is about long-term perseverance.

4. Work in quiet places

Cough!

All it takes is a single noise to break your train of thought, and you have to start regaining your focus from scratch. A small distraction might seem trivial, but can be costly because it can take 5-10 minutes to get back to the level of focus you previously had. And if the distraction is bad enough, it can take you away from your work for hours or even the rest of the day.

If you've ever played in a chess or checkers tournament, you might recall how serious chess and checkers players are possibly some of the most type-A people about keeping the tournament area quiet because every slight noise can break their concentration.

Now picture your work area. Is there outside noise, people talking around you, or even worse for your focus, people stopping by to talk to you?

Be proactive about making your work area as quiet as possible.

Right now, coworking spaces are becoming increasingly popular among entrepreneurs. But co-working spaces with open floor plans can be a killer for your concentration and productivity. You might have previously thought that the most important aspect of your work area is its proximity to the kitchen and bathroom (party animal you!), but arguably the most important thing about your work area is how quiet it is, how few people walk by it, and how inconvenient it is for people to come and bug you. When you need a distraction or a break, you can come to them.

If you are working in an office at a company, you can ask HR or your manager to change where you sit and how you are positioned. Sitting in a quiet area of the office will help you get distracted less often, which will immediately improve your work quality and output quantity.

If you work at a coworking space, choose one with isolated work rooms rather than open floor designs. If you work at home, throw away your TV, and make sure you work in a quiet room of your home or apartment. If you want to be a no-interruption rockstar, you can even choose the neighborhood where you get an apartment or home based on how quiet it is. It might sound like a stretch, but if you primarily work from home and plan to do that for a long time, it will make a world of difference for your focus, concentration, and the eventual quality of what you are working on.

Additionally, if you have family members at home during your work hours or office mates in your office, don't be shy of politely telling them if they are interrupting you. Most of them will be very understanding.

When I was growing up, I did all my homework at home. I had a quiet room, but people barged in at any time. Every time they did that, it would kill my concentration. It was brutal. I had to tell my family that for the next few hours I was busy, but will be available after. That provided a good balance of giving them the time and attention they needed and keeping my work area quiet. Try this tactic if you are in a similar situation.

5. More books, less screens

Did you like my tough love attempt from two sections ago where I told you to discipline yourself? If you were reading the previous section and sarcastically thinking something along the lines of "yes mom" then, my child, I've got a lot more mom stuff for you in this section.

When I coach entrepreneurs, it often feels that I care more about their businesses than they do, and it kills me when they don't put enough effort or apply enough self-discipline when working on their businesses.

Something I notice among my younger clients is that they generally read less, and consume much of their information from quick headlines and soundbites. It is a sign of a decreasing practice of focusing. You must work on improving your ability to focus for longer periods of time, and more intensely. Reading books will help you do that. There are also many mobile app brain training games I'll cover later in this book. You can also learn to play chess which will train you to focus longer and more intensely. Just don't play speed chess. That can actually hurt your ability to focus on one thing for a long period of time. Play the slow and deliberate kind of chess where you are doing a lot of focusing and thinking.

Checkers is a good game too. But all the chess players will make fun of you.

6. Tabs on your browser

I am still laughing after picturing how the chess players will make fun of you if you play checkers. But let's face it, even checkers will be a huge improvement from your current favorite game, Candy Crush. I am having too much fun messing with you. I hope you are finding at least some humor here, and are not offended.

In this section, I have a simple exercise to help boost your focus while working (or playing Candy Crush) at your computer.

The exercise is to minimize the number of tabs that you have open on your browser.

How many browser tabs do you usually have open while working? If I don't discipline myself, I can easily have between 4 and 15 tabs open at a given time. I have two email addresses that I like to check, various analytics I track for my business, including my Amazon author dashboard that shows me my book sales (I love it when people buy my books). After those, I have a few more browser tabs open that I use to do actual work. As you can see I have at least 4 browsers that are pure distractions. That's pretty bad, but many people also have Facebook, Twitter, news, gossip, online shopping, sports and entertainment websites.

The first step is to acknowledge that we have a problem. I am honest. I have this problem. Now, it is your turn. Can you count how many useless tabs you have open? This is your exercise. Like a person on a diet who must track their food intake, your exercise is to track your distracting browser tabs.

The next part of your exercise is to remove at least one useless browser tab from your daily routine. Start small by removing one browser tab, and see how that works for you.

Once you feel comfortable, remove another browser tab. Keep doing that until all your useless browser tabs, or at least as many as you can remove, are gone.

This will help you boost productivity in a small additional way. Removing browser tabs will make your computer work a little faster too.

CHAPTER 4:
PSYCHOLOGY

1. Your subconscious and the story you tell yourself about you

The subconscious is a big part of the productivity puzzle. If you don't improve your productivity and make yourself a more effective professional, underachieving can become your normal, and you will settle on telling yourself that the results you have been getting are the results that you deserve because you are maybe not talented or good enough to get better results.

In other words, poor work habits and poor results will create a low confidence cycle in which you allow yourself to project your poor results into an overall assessment that you make about yourself and where you stand. Before you know it, you may be thinking thoughts like, I am not as smart as I have to be to achieve X, or I am not as creative as I need to be to achieve Y, or no one wants to work with me because of Z.

This negative self-assessment builds subconsciously and reinforces itself as long as you keep achieving poor results.

Making yourself a more productive professional can help you achieve little wins which will naturally begin to reverse your negative self-assessment, and making those little wins can begin by simply turning your work area into a quieter one in which you would have fewer interruptions, have better focus, get more and better work done, and achieve better results.

Better results are the smallest of steps away. But we can convince ourselves that we are where we belong, and not make the necessary changes that can be as simple as switching to working in a quieter place where we will get interrupted less and focus better.

2. Zeigarnik effect

Our brains can be a little strange, especially if you play checkers or Candy Crush. Just kidding about checkers.

One quirk in our brains is explained by the Zeigarnik effect, which is a natural tension we get when we begin working on a task, or if something we are working on isn't at a comfortable stopping point. Having a task that is hanging in the middle makes us feel uncomfortable and pushes us forward towards finishing it.

Before we begin on a task, that task might seem difficult or daunting, and we are more likely to put it off. Once we begin working on that task, the Zeigarnik effect kicks in, and if we stop working on that task, we have a subconscious pull to get back to it and complete it. It gives us momentum and motivation after we've started, and helps to erase the excuses we give ourselves before starting on a task.

3. The discipline of choosing the most important tasks

This theme of choice will recur throughout the book. Just about every chapter will give insights to help you become better at identifying your most important tasks so you don't waste your time focusing on lesser tasks that don't get you closer to your goals.

In this section I want to focus on the psychology of how tasks creep in, and make their way onto your to-do list.

We are greedy. We all want this and that, and we don't want to sacrifice anything to get the things we want. Every time we have an idea, we want to enjoy its benefits. It feels great to add a task to a to-do list, and begin the sweet daydreaming process of imagining ourselves enjoying the benefits of that task, and begin becoming emotionally attached to it. On the other hand, it doesn't feel good to say no to ourselves. To make matters worse, we live in an instant gratification con-sumer-driven culture where we can have almost anything we want at any time, and we practice saying no to ourselves less and less.

This is where you have to be mindful of this process, under-stand how it begins in your mind, and stop it as it begins forming.

You literally have to catch your train of thought before you begin falling in love with new potential benefits you want to get from your new ideas because those new ideas will add extra tasks to your to-do list, and as we already covered, you must be very protective of your to-do list, and not let things creep in there that aren't the most effective at helping you get to your goals.

If you get in the habit of rejecting most ideas that are okay but not great, you will leave your to-do list and your mind uncluttered. Your to-do list will have room for amazing ideas when they come to you, and your mind will have space to roam freely. That free roaming space for your mind will allow it to stumble on better and more creative ideas moving forward.

You must learn to catch yourself before getting overexcited about tasks and subprojects. As you practice discipline and become better at project planning, you will become better at recognizing when the initial excitement is unjustified. You will be able to keep lesser quality tasks off your project list, which will by itself save you weeks if not months of wasted work.

You can use that saved time to become a checkers-master or work on more fruitful projects.

4. Feeling overwhelmed

Everyone feels overwhelmed at some point in their lives. We can feel overwhelmed by having too many things on our to-do list or tight deadlines. You already know not to let too many things creep into your to-do list, but what if they are necessary tasks that can't be taken off your to-do list?

A common way to decrease the feeling of being over-whelmed when facing a big task is to break that task down into a few smaller tasks. You will effectively be making a small project plan for your big task if that big task doesn't already have a project plan. Having a separate to-do list just for the big overwhelming task can often make it easier to manage and work through without feeling as much stress as you would have felt otherwise.

If you feel overwhelmed by a tight deadline, it might be a result of procrastination or poor time management. I'll cover techniques to improve those skills in the future chapters of this book.

CHAPTER 5:
ELIMINATING INTERRUPTIONS

1. The extent of the damage from a single interruption

"It's just one moment," we think. "I will quickly get what I need, and they will go back to work," we think when interrupting people.

Not quite. When a person is focused, they are doing their best work. It isn't easy to get into that focused zone. It takes time and mental effort.

At best, it takes minutes to regain full concentration, and since things are rarely at their best, at worst it leads towards a path of being more distracted by recalling that we have not checked our Facebook in a while, that we need to get coffee and a snack, that we are tired, that the workday is almost over, and that we need to begin wrapping up for the day.

As you can see, every time someone is interrupted, there is a chance that this single interruption will kill productivity for an entire day. It feels innocent, but it is quite damaging.

2. Eliminating interruptions from people online

This might expose me as the curmudgeon that I am, but this is one of my favorite chapters because it's all about telling people to f*** off. Just remember to do so politely, professionally, with a smile, and love, because after all, you should still have love for those people - just not let them interrupt your work.

Let's begin with the biggest culprit of online interruptions: Facebook. That thing is an absolute time sink where your productivity goes to die. If it isn't your friends posting some inflammatory political things you get riled up about, then it's people sending you chat messages about nothing, or even worse, about something relevant for work that isn't as easy to ignore. And if any of those things don't take you away from your work, then cute cat and dog videos will surely distract you.

Personally, I prefer what I call "cat videos 2.0" which are cute interspecies animal videos where animals of different species befriend each other. My latest favorites have been where a baby goat befriended a baby hippo, and where an elephant, tiger and a bear also became friends. As you can see, I am at an advanced level of animal cuteness videos.

For your enjoyment, here is the video where a baby goat becomes friends with a baby hippo:

https://www.youtube.com/watch?v=0bL02GyIsKw

Here is the video about a tiger, bear and a lion becoming friends:

https://www.youtube.com/watch?v=eUg9E41ImzY

True story: as I was getting these links from YouTube, I got distracted watching cute animal videos for about 5 minutes. Ugh.

The best solution is to close the Facebook tab on your browser and to put away your phone while you are working. If you need to use Facebook for work, put whatever tasks require Facebook on your schedule, and only open Facebook when it's scheduled.

Even after you get rid of the Facebook distraction, there are many other places online where people will want to chat with you. There are some common little fibs or truths that you can tell people to help you excuse yourself from those distractions:

- I am heading into a meeting.

- I was on my way out.

- I am busy at the moment.

- Can we chat later? I am overwhelmed with work now.

If all else fails, just allow yourself to have a moment of panic in which you impulsively close the browser tab in which people are chatting with you. You can message people back on your own time when it is convenient for you. Just don't get sucked into a prolonged chat that will be the last thing you do until the next work day.

Once you get a handle on Facebook and chat distractions, there are additional social media distractions coming from sites like Twitter, YouTube, and email. There are tools and apps we'll cover later that will help you control the use of certain websites by blocking them. For now, I understand that telling you to overcome the urge to open Twitter, YouTube, email or other distracting websites isn't enough. But if you get a handle on chat tools and Facebook, you are already ahead of the game!

Next, let's devote a full section just to email.

3. Eliminating email interruptions

The simplest and probably hardest thing to do is to not keep your email open at all times.

To be honest with you, if I had to choose my own biggest productivity problem, I would admit that I have a very hard time not checking email all the time. After all, all kinds of business opportunities could come through email at any moment. Email undermines the level of my focus when I have it open because I keep an eye on it whenever it is open instead of fully focusing on my task at hand.

Imagine if you could improve the quality of your focus by simply not checking email. Imagine how much more work you would get done over the long term, and how much better that work would be.

For me, the realization of how much time I was wasting

checking email was frankly mind-boggling after I realized the full extent of the damage I was causing to myself just by having email open at all times.

So how do you and I solve this problem?

The first step to solving a problem is admitting that you have a problem. It is cheesy but true. After you admit that you have a problem, you will begin to naturally give more attention and a bigger effort towards solving that problem.

If you work with your email, chat, Facebook or other distracting social media or entertainment sites open, let's you and I make a deal: next time we work, we will practice the Pomodoro Technique on that distraction. What I mean by that is if you work with your email open, close it for 20 minutes and after that time open it for 5 minutes. Then do the same thing again and again, slowly increasing your time without email.

Let's do it together! I promise to report on how I did. I'll share my results in the next section of this chapter. I'll write the next section of this chapter after I do at least a few hours of the Pomodoro Technique with my email.

For your part, try the Pomodoro Technique with the source of your biggest online distraction, and send me an email telling me how it worked for you. Here is my personal email address where you can email me and tell me about your experience with this exercise:

alex.genadinik@gmail.com

If you prefer formality, consider this one of the official exercises I give you to practice in this book. But it isn't a required exercise. It's just more fun if we do it together.

Another tip I have to minimize email distractions is to avoid long email thread conversations. They waste a lot of time, distracting you from what you were focusing on with every email you have to open and reply to. If you get into a lot of back and forth with someone on email, invite them to have a quick face to face meeting or a call via phone or Skype. If you continue to use email for correspondence, be brisk in your email messages. That will set the tone for your correspondence partner to also be brisk and to the point. If they are not, politely ask them to keep their messages short. If they persist with the long emails, explain to them that you answer long emails at the end of the week while you can answer short emails quickly. That is a politely veiled threat that you are not going to respond if they write you long emails. Usually, that gets the point across and gets people to communicate more efficiently.

One borderline rude thing I do when getting a very long email is skim it. If I can't understand the major takeaways by skimming, I reply telling the person that I didn't have time to read such a long email and ask them to rephrase it to just a few sentences.

Another tip is to practice not answering your email for a while. This isn't easy for everyone. I experience slight anxiety if I let an email go unanswered for too long. Have you experienced something similar? If you do, practice allowing some emails to just sit there. Instead of dropping everything you are doing and diverting your attention to answering email, if you hold off answering your email to a time that is more convenient for you, you can remain focused on your main tasks and be more productive with them.

Most of the time your email correspondence partners can wait and do not expect you to jump to answer their email. The nature of email is such that the answer doesn't have to come right away.

Some people go as far as purposely waiting until the next day or some long period of time, before answering email. They simply don't want to "train" whoever is emailing them that they are available at all times like a lap dog. They want to create an image that they are a busy professional, and immediately answering email makes them appear as though their time is less valuable than it actually is. Consider this delayed response tactic if you want to make yourself appear independently busy, engaged and of value. Since your time is of value, you can't immediately get to every email. If you can, what does it say about how you value of all your other work?

Granted, the opposite argument is that you want to make your boss, clients, co-workers and family members feel special and valued, and that is why you answer immediately. Plus not answering right away can sometimes lose potential clients because your competitors might answer before you do.

Use your best judgement on when and how fast you answer your email. Just realize that there are advantages and disadvantages to either approach.

4. Results of my "no email" experiment, day one

This is where I put my money where my mouth is, isn't it? I promised to share the results of my own experience closing my email and other distracting browser tabs. Here it is. I am coming clean.

It was a slow and ponderous morning. As I woke up, I asked myself the existential question I've been avoiding for years - can I overcome this problem I have with email having to be open? If it was something easy for me to fix, I would have already done so. But for me, this was a difficult long-term challenge to solve.

It felt a little like I was in an old western movie where two gunslingers were squaring off in a gun battle, both ready to draw their revolvers. I got enough courage to make eye-to-screen contact with my laptop. You'll be proud of me here - I didn't even flinch. Something carried me forward to end up in my chair in one motion right after the eye contact.

It was on. There was no turning back...unless I got a new email I needed to give attention...NO! NOT THIS TIME!

After I moved the TouchPad of my MacBook Pro, the computer "woke up" and just like a gunslinger in an old western, I went bang, bang, bang - closing down all time-wasting programs that I had open from my previous day, starting with email. Then there was quiet. (Old western music playing as you picture the far off mountains beyond the plains with the sun setting and the smoke still coming out of my revolver as it does in old western movies).

I felt naked without my email or social media, but I began to do my work. I was in the unknown. I took the leap.

After a few minutes, I realized that I was okay. It was okay to work like this. I didn't feel bad or good. I simply kept working. It was much more painless than I had imagined. I was immediately more productive and less distracted.

After the first 20 minutes, I checked my email on my phone. Two people had emailed me, and I emailed them back during my break. Then I went back to working with the email closed.

Again, it wasn't bad. I went through a few 20-minute no-email cycles and found myself definitely more focused.

I liked working this way, and for my next step, I made a plan to do at least one hour per day with no-email cycles.

The first day of this experiment turned out better than I thought. I think I may have just gotten myself a new technique to make my work better moving forward. I wonder if I will be able to keep it up.

5. Results of my "no email" experiment, day two

Sorry for all the unnecessary dramatic build-up from the previous section. I didn't initially intend for it to come out that way, but once I started writing, it took on a life of its own. In this section, I'll tell you about day two of my experiment because it wouldn't be a very good experiment if I only tried it once.

Studies show that it takes 2-3 weeks of doing the same thing every day to build a habit, so I wasn't expecting my experiment to have lasting effects after trying it once. But to my surprise, the fear and anxiety that accompanied day 1 weren't there when I sat down to work on the second day. In fact, I even sensed a little bit of a feeling of liberation and freedom. I started the second day with more confidence and comfort.

After I finished my second work day practicing this new no-email strategy, I was trying to figure out where so much comfort and confidence came from after just one work session. The answer I fished out of my brain was that I truly wanted this change for a long time, and looked forward to its positive effects on my productivity and overall business. It was like a new beginning or like seeing a light at the end of the tunnel to solving a problem I've struggled with for a long time, and getting a rejuvenating flood of energy to sprint towards it.

You can probably relate if there is something that has held you back for years that was suddenly gone. Wouldn't it be amazing? That's how it felt for me. Imagine how many hours, weeks and months of productivity have been lost due to that problem in the course of my life. Whatever is holding you back from boosting your productivity, imagine how many promotions or business opportunities it may have caused you to miss out on. Imagine how much money you didn't earn as a result. Now it can all be gone.

That's the hope that was subconsciously giving me the inspiration to make the change. And the change began happening beautifully. I confidently closed email and additional distracting browser tabs. My focus immediately improved because there were less distractions coming from my computer, and I began plowing through my work at a noticeably faster pace than was my norm before. I hope that this happens for you as well.

For you to begin reaping the benefits of improved productivity, you must start implementing the strategies in this book. The book can give you advice, but you have to will yourself to get started and implement the advice. So please don't put it off, and begin implementing and experimenting with the strategies in this book to make them work for you. And if some strategy doesn't immediately work, calibrate and adjust it to make it work for your unique situation.

For your part of this challenge, be honest with yourself and pick something you've been struggling with whether it is checking Facebook, news websites, email or YouTube, and do the same experiment as I did. For your accountability, send me an email and let me know about your results with your experiment. I'll be happy to hear from you. Just picture me cheering you on.

UPDATE: I am updating this section during the editing of this book which happened two months after writing the first draft of this section you just read. While the no-email technique worked initially, like a true addict, I relapsed shortly after and began to work with email open again. I re-tried this experiment several times and relapsed to my prior behavior each time. It took a number of attempts, but at the moment of writing this, I've been good about working without email open, and have kept it up for about a month. The point of this update is that if this doesn't work for you at first, keep trying it and don't give up.

6. Eliminating interruptions from your phone

I hope you don't still have a flip phone or a rotary phone. Just saying.

There isn't much to it when it comes to eliminating distractions from your phone. If it is a smartphone, try keep it on silent and as far from you as possible when you work. If you can keep it in a different room, that is great. If you work in a cubicle where you can't put the phone too far, and if you want a ribbon or a medal from me, keep your phone off for extended periods of time. If you can't get yourself to turn it off, put it to the side with the screen down, or in your bag.

If you are in sales or a customer support position and need to answer your phone as much as possible, you have my blessing to keep the phone turned on and nearby; not that you need my blessing for keeping your phone on, but I thought it was nice of me to give the green light. But even if you need the phone for sales like I sometimes do, it doesn't necessarily mean that you must keep it on and with you at all times. Some people prefer to do video calls on Skype or other voice/video conferencing software. I am one of those people. Skype calls work better for me because it builds more of a relationship than phone communication, and the conversations tend to go better because you can see the other person, their body language, and their facial expressions. Plus, I also try to schedule the call when it will be convenient for me.

That way, my important calls are more personable and possibly more effective, and they get scheduled in my calendar which means that these calls do not interfere with my focus the rest of the day.

If you have a phone that is plugged into a wall and sits on your desk, good luck because it will be a source of unstoppable distractions and desk clutter! Just kidding, unless you truly need it for your work, either keep it unplugged or create a culture with your contacts in which you communicate through email or text, and schedule calls instead of letting people randomly call and distract you. When they call you, it is on their terms. But when you schedule a call, it is on your terms.

Don't let people randomly call you unless it is an emergency, they are clients who can pay you a lot of money, or they are your manager. Train people to schedule calls with you.

I can add that it might also be a good rule to prioritize family communication. Almost everyone else can be trained to make an appointment with you, but your family can be allowed to call you at any time because family is more important than work. Just make sure they don't interrupt you too frivolously. If you plan to turn your phone off, you can give them another way to communicate with you such as Facebook (if other people don't bother you on it), Skype, or whatever you have on during the day where you don't get too many distractions or can designate for family only.

7. Eliminating interriptions from co-workers

What would happen if you were really mean to everyone all the time? Other than being fired from work if you have a 9-5 job, I bet no one would come by to needlessly bother you, and you would get more done.

If you work in an office environment you obviously have co-workers who sometimes come and talk to you. You probably dream of having the office all to yourself, but sadly you share it with others. Plus, since you got this book, I can already tell that you are awesome and that everyone in your office naturally comes over to chat with you because they want to be your friend.

One tactic people use to fend off co-workers who barge into their office or cubicle is using body language that communicates that they are not available to chat at the moment. You can do that by facing towards people with your face, but keeping your hands on your keyboard and your torso still facing your computer. This subconsciously communicates that you are focused on your current task now and can't talk.

Another thing you can do is politely say that you can't chat now, but offer a time to chat later in the day or schedule a small meeting with that person right then and there. You can also ask them when their next break is, and offer to come by their cubicle or office at that time. It's tricky because I know you want to stay "cool" and be their friend, but if you want to keep good focus and illuminate interruptions, you will need at least a little bit of discipline.

I hope you are enjoying this little lesson about how to be "cool" from the biggest nerd out there - me.

8. Eliminating interruptions from your office environment

I've worked in loud offices before, and honestly, when things were loud, I found it very difficult to concentrate well, and was much less effective as an employee. Naturally, my bosses blamed me, and I blamed the noise.

If you have a chance to work in open office spaces or co-working spaces, don't do it!

Every time someone talks to someone else, or someone's phone makes a beeping sound, concentration is broken. A professional should not work like that if their work requires focus and concentration.

One thing some people do is put on noise-canceling head-phones. But even if you can avoid noise distractions by wearing NASA-level noise-canceling headphones, sometimes having people simply walk in front of and behind you can be enough of a distraction.

Another thing that helps some people is to work either late in the evening or very early in the morning because there are fewer people around during those times.

None of these are great solutions. The best solution is to do everything you can not to end up having to work in an environment like that.

If you own your business, the decision of office you will work in is yours, and it is something that is easy to control. If you are an employee at a company, you should tell your boss that working in a loud place is negatively affecting your productivity, and work output. See if there is anything they can do to help you. In the worst case, they might be understanding if your work productivity is lower than it would be if you worked in a quiet place. Of course, they'll still try to blame you in the end, but that's a topic for another book.

CHAPTER 6:
PRODUCTIVITY TOOLS AND APPS

1. Chapter introduction and disclaimer

I want to start with a disclaimer and a full disclosure about the tools I'll be recommending. This already sounds fishy, doesn't it? If you are thinking to yourself "yes it does" then stop thinking that! I was just joking. This is a way for me to be honest about why some software and apps appear on the recommended list so that you don't think that I was paid to add any of them to this chapter.

Disclaimer and full disclosure: I only share software tools and apps in this section that I believe they will help you. I am not in a business relationship with any of the apps that will be mentioned in this section other than:

1) Business apps I made which I will mention
2) Udemy app. I am not paid or reimbursed in any way by Udemy for promoting their app. Although I do have a business relationship with them because I am a publisher of courses on their website. I happen to offer a gift to readers of this book which is one free course of mine of your choosing. I explain how to see the full list of courses

and get yours for free at the end of the book. These courses are hosted on the Udemy website.

2. Google Calendar

I realize that this is a very common app, and you don't need me to officially suggest it in a book, but hey, I already did.

I am mentioning this app first because by this point in the book it should be clear that we must take control of our schedules in order to give our important tasks the proper focus and attention. If you are not already using a calendar app, a scheduling tool, or some pen and paper dinosaur way of maintaining your schedule, at least start thinking about it or just get the calendar app. It's free and easy to install in just a minute.

If you don't already keep a calendar, is it because you don't want to become a Type A person who sweats the small stuff, and has a compulsive need to plan everything? To be honest, that was originally my hesitation too. I didn't want myself to one day look in the mirror and have a Kafkaesque experience of being shocked by the Type A person I've become.

What eventually made me come to terms with keeping a calendar is that it was going to make it easier for me to discipline myself and help me become a more effective professional, which would help me grow my business faster. Ironically, growing your business faster would help you get to a point when you can hire an assistant to maintain your calendar for you. They can take over the Type A responsibilities.

Keeping a calendar will help you organize your tasks and

help you manage your time better. Time management and organization are productivity strategies we will explore later in this book. Most successful professionals and managers keep a calendar. In addition to helping them stay organized, it also helps them plan their days and weeks in a way that helps them avoid low potential tasks creeping into their schedules.

Here is the Google Calendar app for the iPhone:

https://itunes.apple.com/us/app/google-calendar-make-most/id909319292?mt=8

(Shortened link: https://goo.gl/3miU8b)

Here is the Google Calendar app on Android:

https://play.google.com/store/apps/de-tails?id=com.google.android.calendar&hl=en

(Shortened link: https://goo.gl/DU8Aa5)

3. To-do note-taking apps

I love these things!

When I am on the go and I have an idea, I write that idea on my note-taking app. Of course, what you write down is only great if you remember to come back and check what you wrote. Admittedly, I sometimes forget to check what I wrote in my to-do apps when I am making my work to-do lists or project plans.

I especially love using note-taking apps on train or bus rides, or when I have idle time. I let my creative and strategic thinking go to work, and can write it all down in the app. If you actually come back and check what you wrote in the app, it will help you remember some of your best ideas. Even if you forget to check what you wrote, the process of writing ideas down in the app will help you remember them, and incorporate them into your overall vision and strategy.

Here is my favorite simple note-taking app on Android called Color NotePad Notes:

https://play.google.com/store/apps/details?id=com.social-nmobile.dictapps.notepad.color.note&hl=en

(Shortened link: https://goo.gl/Ftczid)

Here is a similar app (not the same developer) on iPhone called Color Notes:

https://itunes.apple.com/us/app/color-notes/id830515136?mt=8

(Shortened link: https://goo.gl/moRk7H)

4. Proper ways to make to-do lists

Some people make the mistake of writing down one big task in their to-do list, and having it read like "work on my business" which is a big and daunting task when you are about to sit down to work on your business. Plus, it isn't helpful because you already know that you are supposed to work on your business.

Instead of writing things in the to-do list as one or a few large items which will seem daunting and may contribute to your procrastination by being too overwhelming to start, try to break the big tasks like the endless "work on my business" task into many smaller tasks.

Here is an example of my to-do list for tomorrow:

- Post business promotions on Facebook groups

- Email book promotion sites with a pitch for my book

- Follow up with company x about a partnership

- Reply to questions posted on my app

- Record a YouTube video on business planning

- Send an email promotion for my online courses

- Tidy up my work area

- Continue writing the long blog post that I've been working on

Writing down small tasks helps you quickly accomplish them and build momentum. If you ever play video games, there is a similarity in how they make you feel after getting points and leveling up to accomplishing tasks on your to-do lists.

Research has shown that accomplishing little wins in video games helps release endorphins, makes you feel better, and gets you to continue playing by making you feel good during game play. The same thing happens when you accomplish work tasks. If you break a big task into many easy small tasks, it will get you to keep accomplishing little wins, make you feel better, see tangible progress, and continue playing the game of your business.

As a side note, if you do play video games, I am looking for good recommendations for mobile apps games. Please send recommendations my way however ironic this request may be from an author of a productivity book.

5. Trello for team productivity

The Trello app is useful when managing a team or delegating tasks to freelancers.

If you run a 1-person business, this app isn't that useful. Just take it as a compliment that I believe in your ability to one day grow your business to have a team, and skip ahead to the next section.

If you do have a team, this project management software will allow you to see what everyone is working on, monitor everyone's progress and effectiveness, and delegate tasks more intelligently because you will have a better sense of where everyone is in accomplishing tasks currently assigned to them.

It also makes it easier to spot slackers.

Link to the Trello website:

https://trello.com/

6. Podcasting apps to help you learn on the go

I am about to intrude on a big part of your day. If you are still reading and have not sent me hate email about my other suggestions or bad jokes, perhaps you won't mind the intrusion. What I am about to suggest is something that I already do to myself. When I walk anywhere, commute, or do many kinds of exercise that range from running to stationary bikes, to elliptical machines, I often listen to podcasts.

If you are like most people, these activities take up many hours of your week, making this potentially substantial.

Download a podcasting app, and explore podcasts on all kinds of topics and professional interests that can help you in whatever you are working on. By doing so, you can transform the time you don't usually use to boost your business, and turn it into time you can use to learn new strategies and ideas.

I have listened to podcasts for years, and can honestly say that I would not have made nearly as much progress in my business without everything I've learned from podcasts. Years ago when I was struggling to find the right business strategies for my company, I listened to Jason Calacanis and his "This Week In Start-ups" podcast. After that, when I made my first app, I listened to Steve P. Young's "Mobile App Chat" podcast which has been renamed to "App Masters" podcast. After I was able to grow my own mobile apps and make them a success, I was invited to be a guest to be interviewed on the AppMasters.co podcast twice on different occasions. After I began promoting my business on YouTube, I listened to different YouTube podcasts which gave me the knowledge that I was able to apply to make my videos more successful and grow my YouTube channel.

There were many more podcasts that helped me. As I moved forward with my business and needed to learn new things, there seemed to always be some podcasts that covered that subject matter. Podcasts can help you in exactly the same way.

Podcasts are free and they offer thousands of combined hours of learning that don't have to take away a minute of your work time!

And what was the reason for me informing you about podcasts on which I've been interviewed? So that you would see how awesome I am. No, before you begin thinking that I am pompous in addition to not funny, that was a joke - so still, just not funny. The real reason I told you about the podcasts I've been on is to illustrate a further productivity point. You can easily reach out to podcast hosts. If you are a fan, the hosts will appreciate that, and if you keep in touch with the hosts, and eventually do something noteworthy with your business, you might get invited to be a guest, and get promotion for your business from the same podcasts you've been learning from.

The result is countless free hours of learning, and potential business relationships and promotion for your business, all for listening to podcasts.

Podcasting app I use on Android:

https://play.google.com/store/apps/details?id=com.bam-buna.podcastaddict&hl=en

(Shortened link: https://goo.gl/kff1BR)

Podcasts app on the iPhone:

https://itunes.apple.com/us/app/pod-casts/id525463029?mt=8

(Shortened link: https://goo.gl/q9J55F)

7. Udemy app to learn on the go

Udemy is a website that provides video-based courses. I teach many courses there and take many courses as a student as well.

You can download their mobile app, and watch the courses on your commute, while riding a stationary bike at the gym, or during idle time. Many of the courses are theoretical so you can listen to them just like you would listen to a podcast. If you have a limit on your phone's data plan, you can connect using Wi-Fi and download course lectures that will be available to listen to at any later time.

When comparing podcasts to courses, the quality of learning in courses is considerably higher because they are specifically designed to help you learn. The advantage of podcasts is that they are free. Courses are typically not free, but you can often buy them for as little as $10 on promotions. For the value of learning something amazing or professionally useful that price is a steal.

Between listening to the podcasts and watching Udemy courses, you might end up spending more time on the treadmill and the stationary bike, and fall in love with your commute. You are welcome for that! Of course, if you feel that you get value from this book, and if you ever do want to thank me, the best way is to write a nice review for this book on Amazon. I would REALLY appreciate it.

Udemy app for Android:

https://play.google.com/store/apps/details?id=com.udemy.android&hl=en

(Shortened link: https://goo.gl/Ycvqsb)

Udemy app for iPhone:

https://itunes.apple.com/us/app/udemy-online-courses/id562413829?mt=8

(Shortened link: https://goo.gl/NOjjN7)

8. Pocket app for bookmarking

Pocket is a popular and simple app. If you are browsing anything, you can bookmark it with this app, and come back to that content later. That's it. It will help you remember to come back to interesting and useful content, and will even recommend additional content based on the things you've bookmarked.

Pocket app for Android:

https://play.google.com/store/apps/details?id=com.ideashower.readitlater.pro&hl=en

(Shortened link: https://goo.gl/vNekM2)

Pocket app for iPhone:

https://itunes.apple.com/us/app/pocket-save-articles-videos/id309601447?mt=8

(Shortened link: https://goo.gl/qRgM27)

9. TimeSink app

Joke about you not realizing how much time you waste goes here.

Unfortunately, despite the joke potential of the subject matter, I can't think of a really awesome one at the moment.

But I didn't give up on coming up with an amazing joke. I took a mental break, checked Facebook, Twitter, email, a few of my favorite apps, then email again, then back to Facebook to answer a chat message, and now I am back to writing in just 2 minutes. Or was it 20 minutes? Maybe it was closer to 30 minutes that felt like only a few.

Want to have a better understanding of what websites you waste your time on, and how much total time you lose daily?

TimeSink can help you with that. This software tracks the programs you have open, and for how long you had them open throughout the day. Knowing this will help you understand how much time you waste during the day, and on what. You can use other software to block sites where you waste the most time, and hopefully diminish the damage to your productivity caused by some of your web surfing.

TimeSink is a paid (but cheap) software package. Here is the link to get it from the Apple App Store:

https://itunes.apple.com/us/app/time-sink/id404363161?mt=12

(Shortened URL: https://goo.gl/A0irLh)

10. Software that blocks Facebook and time wasting websites

There is a whole class of software that blocks access to certain websites for a temporary amount of time. This is useful for us once we identify which websites waste most of our time so we can block those websites. Of course, having many similar software companies that built essentially the same software begs the question of why so many people built the same thing? Couldn't they try to be more original?

These copycat software packages can be set to block sites like Facebook, or any other sites you tell it to block. Blocking sites can help you discipline yourself if you can't stay off those sites on your own.

Of course, the one important thing none of these software programs have figured out is how will you find the discipline to use their Facebook blocking software if you don't have the discipline to close Facebook on your own.

Here is an example of software that can help you block applications on PC or Mac:

https://focusme.com/

11.Pomodoro app

I don't know about you, but I got all Pomodoro'd out back in Chapters One and Two. I added the Pomodoro app to this list because it is a classic productivity app, and if it wasn't in this list, someone would inevitably ask me why I didn't add it after recommending the Pomodoro Technique. For those people who would have asked me about it, here you go, I added it to the list of productivity apps.

The Pomodoro app is a time tracking app which alerts you when your periods of work and breaks begin and end. It is slightly more useful than simply looking at your watch and keeping track of time on your own.

Here is one of the Pomodoro apps for Android (there are many similar apps that essentially do the same thing since it is a pretty basic app):

https://play.google.com/store/apps/details?id=com.tat-kovlab.pomodorolite&hl=en

(Shortened URL: https://goo.gl/3STaWI)

Here is a Pomodoro app for iOS:

https://itunes.apple.com/us/app/pomodoro-time-focus-timer/id973134470?mt=12

(Shortened URL: https://goo.gl/nG0thR)

12.Boomerang app for Gmail (Chrome extension)

The Boomerang app helps you keep track of important email

threads. We all sometimes forget to follow up on email conversations if we don't hear back from people for too long. That causes many conversations to simply stop and dissolve.

If you prevent ongoing conversations from dropping, it can result in stronger business relationships, more sales, potential jobs or clients, or partnerships.

Here is the link for the Chrome App Store since this is a Chrome extension:

https://play.google.com/store/apps/details?id=com.baydin.boomerang&hl=en

(Shortened URL: https://goo.gl/nG8MUq)

13. Social Quant and SocialOomph

In this section, I'll cover two apps that work well together to automate your social media marketing, namely Twitter.

Social Quant works by having you tell it what business niche or industry you are in and finding people for you to follow on Twitter who are in your industry or similar interest areas. As this software follows people for you, some of those people will follow you back, and you will grow your Twitter followers.

SocialOomph works by letting you preload many tweets (possibly hundreds or thousands) that it will automatically tweet out at a time interval that you set. It will continue to cycle through the list of tweets you give it until the list is done, at which time it will start from the top of the list.

By using these two tools, every day you will have more followers on Twitter who might see your tweets, click on links in them, and possibly buy your products. The best part about using these is that it will almost entirely automate your Twitter marketing. Other than occasionally having to check who might be tweeting at you, or preload more tweets, these tools will allow you to be almost entirely hands-off with your Twitter marketing.

You can also supercharge this Twitter marketing strategy by setting up your LinkedIn profile to update with your Twitter updates.

Link to SocialQuant's website:

https://www.socialquant.net

Link to SocialOomph website:

https://www.socialoomph.com/

14. Brain training games to increase productivity

If you are on the go but don't have time to listen to full podcast episodes or take Udemy courses, you can play games. No, you can't play your favorite Candy Crush. I want you to play nerdy, brain training games. There are many such games available for free. They can train your memory, logic and other common tasks that you use professionally and in daily life.

If you have just five minutes to "waste" somewhere, and don't want to waste them, you can play these games.

Funny update and potential TMI alert: after an early test reader (this is a person who gets an early draft of the book to provide feedback) of this book read the previous sentence, he said that the perfect place to play these games is on the toilet which is where you have a few minutes to "waste." Waste - terrible pun, isn't it? To that I say: if it makes you more productive, I am all for it.

Also on my approved list are chess and checkers games (either as a board game or on your phone) because they also help to train your mind.

Popular brain training game app on Android which is free:

https://play.google.com/store/apps/details?id=godlinestudios.brain.training&hl=en

(Shortened URL: https://goo.gl/KIv0sQ)

Popular brain training game on iPhone which is free:

https://itunes.apple.com/us/app/elevate-brain-training/id875063456?mt=8

(Shortened URL: https://goo.gl/OapMza)

15. Headspace mindfulness app

If I have not sufficiently intruded on your life, this might be the last straw. I'm about to suggest that you try meditation. If you think I am crazy, why has it taken you this long to get it? Shouldn't it have been obvious from chapter one?

Where was I? Meditation.

Why am I suggesting meditation in a productivity book? If a person isn't in touch with themselves, they might not be fully aware of the purpose of their life, often mistaking life purpose with the act of choosing what to pursue on a daily, weekly and long-term basis.

With this in mind, let me ask you: if you are extremely productive working on something that can be called a mis-goal or a misdirection in your life, how productive are you really? An argument can be made that 100% of the work a person did to get to their mis-goal was wasted, and was 100% NOT productive. A counter-argument is that even if you worked on a mis-goal, you still learned a lot during your work, and got experience. So not everything was wasted. The eventual agreement may be that despite learning and getting other benefits from working on your mis-goals, you made very little progress towards your real goals, and it can be concluded that you were quite unproductive if not entirely so.

Imagine if you were pursuing your mis-goals for months or even years. That's an unbelievable waste. Let's make sure that this never happens, and that you begin to understand your inner self better as fast as possible.

Meditation is an amazing tool to help you get there. There are many different types of meditation. Later in this book we'll focus on Mindfulness Meditation and basic self-awareness. This section just focuses on apps and tools for it.

Headspace is a free popular app that can help you learn how to meditate. Here is the link to a landing page from which you can get either the Android, iPhone or the Amazon version of that app:

https://www.headspace.com/headspace-meditation-app

16. My own Problemio.com apps that help you start a business

I left the apps dearest to my heart for last. These are the apps I built, which helped me gain broad insight into entrepreneurship, and were the start to the business I run today.

The apps now come as a 4-app "course" on Android and iPhone. This 4-app series takes you from business ideas to business planning to raising money to marketing your business. How I built the apps is of interest so I'll briefly share that.

In the early versions of the apps, I added one feature which made all the difference. That feature allowed app users to ask me business questions for free. Over time, thousands of entrepreneurs asked me business questions. I already had significant business experience before these apps, but through helping countless of entrepreneurs on my apps, I gained a lot more insight into the entrepreneurial experience.

After 300,000 people used the apps, I collected all their questions from my database, and answered those questions in my first book (while preserving people's privacy of course). Luckily, not all of the 300,000 initial app users asked me questions because if they did, I would still be sitting there, typing out answers.

I still talk to entrepreneurs as a part of my coaching practice and when I support people who buy my paid products. The number of entrepreneurs I've coached is growing daily.

If you are wondering whether you can still ask me business questions through the app, the answer is no. I am currently in the process of phasing that feature out because it is no longer efficient for me to type out answers on the phone.

Instead, I offer paid coaching on Skype. As a thank you for getting this book, one of the FREE gifts I offer you at the end of the book is a little bit of personalized help. You are welcome to email me with your questions. You can read about the details of how to get in touch with me, along with other freebies at the end of this book.

Here are the links to get my free apps to help you in generating business ideas, business planning, fundraising and marketing.

Free Android business plan app:

https://goo.gl/GDl0TB

Free Android marketing app:

https://goo.gl/jhsWt6

Free Android app on fundraising and making money:

https://goo.gl/BcAX60

Free business idea Android app:

https://goo.gl/niEjaH

Free business idea iPhone app:

https://goo.gl/eyKEzT

Free iPhone business plan app:

https://goo.gl/VBWtsC

Free iPhone marketing app:

https://goo.gl/8I112P

Free iPhone app for fundraising:

https://goo.gl/WO1L53

CHAPTER 7:
ORGANIZING YOUR WORK
ENVIRONMENT

1. Chapter introduction

Are you messy? Admit it! It's OK if you are. Only this book will witness your confession. This book and YOU as you hear the truth reverberate in your soul.

I just went to a dark place, didn't I? I wanted to kick off this section with a bang since for many people, organization isn't the most exciting field of productivity. Organization is that sneaky part of productivity, the benefit of which is reaped largely subconsciously. If you are more organized, it quietly helps your day and your work go smoothly. If you are not organized, your days become more haphazard, stressful and hectic, often without you realizing why that is.

Let's give organization the necessary attention it deserves. Apply a few easy tactics, and hopefully reap its disproportionately awesome benefits.

2. Philosophy of "item groups" with everything having its designated place

Calling this a philosophy probably made Socrates and Aristotle spin in their graves. I'd say sorry to them, but why single out a small group of real philosophers to apologize to after I angered so many more people with my bad jokes throughout this book.

Do you ever lose your keys in your own home, and spend stressful minutes or hours frantically digging through your entire place before you had to leave?

You probably don't have this experience often because after the first few times this happened you figured out that if you just put your keys in a specific place every time you got home, you would be able to find them there when you need them. This section is about applying this simple paradigm to things you commonly use in your work.

Exercise: for this exercise, you will need to group the items that you use for work. Some examples of groups are checks and personal finances like bills, tax records, project plans, office supplies, and small tech gadgets and batteries.

Having a designated place for a group of items makes them easy to find and keeps your desk uncluttered since every group will be put in its natural storage place.

To start the exercise take a sheet of scratch paper and write down the "groups" of things you use for work. For my overachievers out there, if you've come up with 20 or 100 groups for things, you've gone too far. Keep it simple with no more than 5-10 major groups. If you see one group getting too large, you can break it up into two logical groups to make that big group more organized.

Once you've written down enough groups, go through your work area and assign each item in your work area to a group. For example, a pen would get assigned to an office supplies group, and a random piece of mail would get assigned to a group designed for mail to be answered. That will create a chart (actually a tree graph if we want to be algorithmically accurate) of everything you use with their proper grouping.

Once you have everything grouped, you will need to determine the appropriate storage option and storage arrangement. I'll go over many storage options shortly.

After you have everything grouped and stored accordingly, you should have significantly fewer instances where you waste time by digging through your entire work area or even worse your entire home, looking for something. Your work area will also be immediately more organized, and you will have a clearer focus thanks to the boost in organization and decrease of clutter.

3. 4 types of organizers and shelves for storage

In this section I will share a few types of inexpensive organizers and cabinets that you can use in your office or home, and for placing things into the designated group areas we discussed in the previous section.

The first type of organizer is a legal filing cabinet. This is something that I use at home. Depending on the types of desk you have, these can sometimes be tucked right under each side of your desk without taking up any space in your office environment. I have two of these in my work area. One on the right side of my desk, and one on the left. They immediately give me 4 large areas to put the things I use for work. What I really like about this setup is that I can reach any of the 4 large areas without having to get up. This keeps my distractions to a minimum.

If you don't want such bulky metallic items in your office space, you can get basket organizers as shown below. They have a more pleasant appearance, and they can be placed on many different kinds of shelves or storage units in flexible arrangements.

Here is an example of an inexpensive shelf organizer inside which you can put many different baskets of different sizes. Such organizers can be taller and wider with more areas for putting things into them. A way to make your work area immediately more pleasant is to put a nice plant into one of the squares of this type of shelf.

There are also see-through, pull-out shelf organizers. The example here is probably overkill with way too many storage units, but you can use this kind of item to store things of different sizes.

4. Desk organizers

Everyone is familiar with desk organizers. What I'll do in this section is briefly introduce a couple of available types of desk organizers to give you a sense of what there is to choose from, and quickly move on to the next section of this book.

The first type of desk organizer is useful if you are an office supplies geek like I am, and you have too many post-it notes and pens lying around.

If you have many files, letters or different kinds of paper-work on your desk, here is a type of file organizer that might be more suitable for you.

5. Whiteboard

Nothing gives me a sweeter false sense of intelligence than a nice, BIG whiteboard on which I can draw up ideas and connect them with strategic arrows.

I love it when a good arrow gets placed between two barely related items. If you are looking for true business secrets, it's having the skill to draw awe-inspiring arrows after which the chaotic universe suddenly makes sense. That was probably one too many jokes about arrows, but you will see my point when you have your whiteboard with your own ideas and awesome arrows.

If we can be serious for a second, having a whiteboard helps you put big ideas "on paper" and plan their nuances in a more organized manner. Having your ideas and plans visually represented also gives you a way to revisit them, and rethink fine points of your strategies.

To illustrate the boost from visualization, let's use a chess analogy. If you think about a chess move for only 10-20 seconds, that move will have a high chance to be a mistake. At best, it will be ill-conceived. But if you stare at the chessboard for 5-10 minutes you will likely see all the blunders, and give yourself a chance to make a much more effective move after thinking through many possibilities.

Now imagine playing chess without the board. It would be much more difficult to think ahead because you would forget where all the other pieces are after just a handful of moves. Seeing the pieces visually represented on the board helps you come back to the current situation and think from that solid starting point. That's what a whiteboard gives you.

Imagine if you stared at the chessboard daily for 5-10 minutes. Not only would you have thought about your move for hours, but you would also give your brain a chance to process and work on the situation during idle time.

If you do this, chances are that as a chess player, you will make moves that are far superior. That is what a simple whiteboard gives you if you buy one, hang it in your work area, and use it as it is meant to be used (to draw awesome arrows).

With a whiteboard, the strength of your ideas is equivalent

to a chess player who has been thinking about their best move for days. Without a whiteboard, you are like a chess player that doesn't even have a board. Which player do you think would win?

Pro tip: while you are shopping for a whiteboard, don't forget to buy markers. If you forget to buy markers, you will have a "duh" moment when you get home.

6. Sharing my own work experience

We've been going over some theory. I want to add a practical example. In this section, I'll share a case study of my own home office environment.

On the right side behind me I have a recycling bin, and on the left side behind me, I have a garbage bin. Yes, I am a nerd with two waste bins, but I feel good about recycling. Having an easy way to separate trash from recycling helps me prevent clutter from accumulating on my desk.

On the left wall behind me, I have a 12-months paper calendar that I flip every month. Keeping one of those calendars is a bit old school of me. No one seems to keep those anymore. I like to make notes in it and flip through it at the end of the year to see my progress, reflect on everything I've worked on, and see which of those things moved my life and work forward so I can do more of that in the future.

On the wall to my right, I have a big whiteboard which is waiting for my next big ideas and awesome arrows. Further behind me, I have a small stretching area where I take little breaks since sitting in one place for too long is bad for you.

114

I recently bought a standing desk that doubles as a stationary bike on which I can exercise while working. I'll show it to you in another section of this chapter.

On the left side of my desk in front of me, I have a big window from which I get natural sunlight, and on the right side of my desk I have some storage bins for extra organization.

Under my desk are pull-out drawers for storing documents and small tech gadgets, and office supplies. Each of these groups of things has their own place, so I never waste time or mental energy looking for lost items.

On the opposite side of my desk across from where I usually sit, I have a green screen that I use as a professional (amateur) background for recording video. It is permanently set up next to the back wall so it doesn't take up much room. Since it doesn't take up much room, I never take it down after filming and don't need to assemble it back up when I want to start filming. Any time I need to record video, I just point the camera at it, sit on the opposite side of my desk, and voila! I am in a professional (amateur) video recording studio. When I am done recording, I just go back to the original side of my desk and resume regular work.

In the next section I'll cover some ideas for interesting and unique desks, and after that we'll discuss the space on the immediate top of your desk

7. Standing desks

Standing desks have less to do with productivity, and more to do directly with your health.

Sitting for extended periods of time is very bad for you. Many people who work office jobs develop major back problems by their late 20s or mid-30s even if they are otherwise healthy. People whose jobs don't require sitting for extended periods of time develop back problems at a much lower rate.

The old man writing this book who is in his mid 30's, me, has had some pretty bad back injuries due to mostly sitting at work. Who knew that sitting is such back-breaking work. Don't be like me. After I had to go to physical therapy, my physical therapist advised me to get a standing desk. That's advice from a healthcare professional, not me. Plus, standing burns more calories than sitting.

Standing desks help you preserve your health longer, and burn more calories. Consider investing in one for at least a part of your work.

Here is one that I bought which is a standing desk and a stationary bike at the same time. This isn't me in the picture below. That's a photo I found online.

Here is a standing desk that can also double as a treadmill on which you can walk (also not me in the photo):

You can also get a standing desk that is just a standing desk without a bike or a treadmill attached to it. Most standing desks fold up to double as a sitting and standing desk so you can use the same desk for sitting and standing.

If you use an exercise desk that is either also a treadmill or a stationary bike, and spend an hour or two on it per day, depending on your exercise needs, you may be able to skip some trips to the gym or quit the gym entirely which would save you a significant amount of money and time.

If you can put that money and time back into your business,

that will result in a very significant productivity boost.

8. The top of your desk

I like to keep an ample amount of scratch paper for idea exploration and spur of the moment ideas and plans. I keep the paper in the area on my desk that is in front of me, and slightly to the right since I am right-handed.

If you are left-handed, I'll let it slide if you use the area on your desk that is slightly to your left.

The paper I use is exclusively scratch paper or the back of junk mail. I try to not use any new paper because I have delusions that this small effort of mine will somehow help the environment be less ruined. I realize that this futile effort won't make a difference, but it makes me feel good.

Why do I do these things to myself, I don't know. But I am sure some rude person will inform me why and how I am an idiot in the Amazon book reviews. Thanks to that wonderful person in advance. Feel welcome to defend my recycling habits by balancing out the negative reviews with a positive one of your own.

Having extra scratch paper does not clutter up my desk because I have a specific place for storing it. I also do my best to keep only one sheet of it on my desk at all times.

To aid creativity, do your best to remove as many items as possible from the top of your desk. Clutter restricts you mentally and physically. Use the strategies in previous sections to declutter your desk by putting items into groups and those groups into their dedicated storage areas.

My goal is always to have only my laptop, glass of water, pen and scratch paper on my desk, but as much as I try to declutter the top of my desk, it is a constant struggle. Things seem to want to end up there.

Mistakes I am prone to making:

- Eating at my desk and then letting the empty plate sit on top of the desk for too long to admit. Gross, I know, but when I am in the middle of a heated workday, it is not always easy or most constructive to focus on tidying up my desk.

- Letting extra papers with notes linger on my desk for days because each paper may have notes pertaining to different sub projects, tasks, or new potential initiatives.

One thing many people like is having multiple monitors on their desk. For some people it is great. Personally I find it distracting since it is often best to focus on one thing at a time. But you have my blessing on this one.

9. Lighting: What types and how much

Studies show that people work better and more creatively with natural sunlight. Here are all the lighting variations in order from worst to best:

- Working in darkness

- Working in dim light

- Working in a regularly lit room with fluorescent light

- Working in an office that gets natural light from the sun

- Sitting near an unshaded window and getting natural sunlight

Natural sunlight can improve your mood, increase feelings of happiness, make you more alert, and with all those things, more ready to work and more productive.

10. Wireless devices: keyboard, mouse, etc

Wires from electronics like your computer, monitor, mouse, mobile phone charger and other devices can quickly clutter a work area.

I recommend investing in wireless devices as much as possible. The most common wireless devices are wireless mouse, wireless keyboard, wireless headphones, and connecting to the Internet via Wi-Fi instead of an ethernet cable.

If you charge your phone or any other device on your desk, consider using power outlets that are further away. Doing this will declutter your desk, make your work area more pleasant, and help you decrease distractions from your phone and the other devices since they will be far away.

If you are worried that the universe will come off its axis if you don't immediately jump to respond to phone messages, just look on the bright side that a delay in responding will give you more time to choose the most fitting and witty emoticons to use in your replies.

11.Philosophy of having everything a reach away

Here I go irritating Plato and Aristotle again with my liberal use of the word philosophy. The "everything within reach" strategy organizes your work area so that everything you need in your daily work is just a reach away. This helps minimize the interruptions that happen when you have to get up to get what you need.

Let's consider an example of when you need to staple something. If a stapler is a reach away, it takes you 5 seconds to reach for it, staple something, and resume your work. If the stapler is not a reach away, you have to stand up and walk over to where the stapler is or even worse, search for the stapler. This not only takes more time but destroys your momentum. What if you have to ask someone where the stapler is, or for permission to use theirs? This unnecessary interaction can turn into a longer conversation and kill many more minutes.

When working this way, people often have no idea where the time goes. That's because it is wasted on little interruptions that turn into bigger wastes of time which can be avoided. It is better to have that stapler a reach away, and never have to think twice about it. The time saving of having something a reach away vs. not having it can immense and very underrated.

12.Cleaning wipes for electronics

If you ever have your boyfriend or girlfriend over, and you pull up a laptop to see some YouTube video or show them something on social media, and your laptop screen and keyboard are dirty or dusty, that will put a damper on your love life that day.

When I suggest that you buy cleaning wipes to wipe down your work area, your keyboard, and your laptop screen, I am not only helping you organize your work area and have less germs on your computer, but I am also helping your romantic life. Thank me later (or better now with an Amazon review of this book)!

For many examples of cleaning wipes you can get, search Amazon or Google for "antibacterial cleaning wipes for keyboard or computer screen" and you will find many suitable results.

13. Should you eat at your desk?

I like to eat at my desk. It is a pretty bad and gross habit. It may be my biggest vice in terms of how I work. The surface of your desk, your keyboard, and your mouse or laptop trackpad have more germs than your toilet seat. It is very unsanitary to eat there, and touch your food using the hands that touch your trackpad and keyboard.

Another problem with eating at your desk is that eating becomes mindless. You mindlessly shove food in your mouth while you focus on working, and you don't focus on tasting and enjoying your food. Not only does this prevent you from developing a more refined taste for food like the refined devil you have potential to be, but this is the surest way to gain weight. People who eat while working typically eat more per meal because they aren't sensible about how much they eat. They just gobble it up. Eating at your desk can often get you to eat faster than you usually would, which means that you would eat more before you feel full. Additionally, if you eat at your desk, you are often stress eating, which can also cause you to gobble up unnecessary calories.

The only way to keep your weight off after regularly over-eating at your desk is to exercise more, and that extra exercise will take up extra hours every week, which are hours you could have spent being productive with something important.

Overeating and overcompensating for it at the gym can turn into an endless, time-sucking cycle at the end of which you will turn yourself into a good athlete. The problem is that your goal wasn't to become a good athlete. It was to work better. Does this sound like your experience, or like someone you might know? I've certainly been guilty of this. It can be avoided by being more mindful about your eating and managing it instead of having it control you.

Be mindful of your every meal, keep it reasonable and don't use food to cope with stress. By doing this you will still have a better chance of staying fit, and save a tremendous amount of time. Your productivity will be boosted from the extra time you will be able to devote to your work instead of the gym.

14. Exercise 1 for organization: Spend 5 minutes daily on organizing

People often ask for exercises in how-to books. I always wonder whether people actually do those exercises. I came up with an exercise that will teach you a lesson to never ask for an exercise again - cleaning.

Try to allocate (or add to your calendar if you are amazing and are following the tips in this book by using a calendar) 5 minutes each day for tidying up and organizing your work area. The best time for tidying up is right before the last task of your work day. Cleaning at this time not only ensures that you will start off the next day with a clean and organized work space, but also that you won't put it off because you want to go home

Try this for 30 days in a row in an effort to make this a habit.

15. Exercise 2 for organization: create a to-do space

If you are like most people, when you have bills or documents you receive in the mail, if they require any real effort, you probably leave it to do later, forget about it, and the document or bill gets neglected and forgotten, resulting in late fees or other unpleasantries.

This happens to many people. One way to get a handle on it is to have a specific area designated for mail or tasks that need to be completed. Remember when you created groups of things earlier in this chapter? One of the groups should be a to-do group. Spending few minutes a day cleaning out the to-do group by working on whatever gets into it will help decrease your lateness on addressing those tasks and documents, and keep you from getting in trouble.

For your exercise:

1) Create a to-do area
2) Spend 5 minutes per day working on things that are in your to-do area
3) Do this for 30 days in a row to make it a habit

You can do this exercise every day after you complete the exercise from the previous section. That's only 10 minutes per day to get a tremendous boost in organization and productivity.

Plus, if any of your to-do items require you to pull up information or tools, you should be able to easily find that information or tools because everything you need will be a reach away if you followed the "everything a hand reach away" philosophy (hi Plato!) from earlier in this chapter.

16. One more point about not eating at your desk

Since I struggle with this issue and so do many other people, let's bring this disgusting-ness to the forefront of our attention to hopefully resonate in all of our minds, and deter us from eating at our desk, instantly making us healthier. Remember, our health has a direct correlation with our ability to be productive long-term. If we get sick, we can't work at all.

You are what you eat. When you eat at your desk, you eat more germs and nasty bacteria that live on everything you touch with your hands which you then use to touch your food.

That immediately makes all of you less healthy. Your immune system will suffer, your hair will have less shine, your skin less smooth, and god knows what will happen inside your body.

How is that for a scare tactic? Did I get you to freak out? I know I got myself to freak out a little bit. Writing it is helping to make this issue more real for me, and I am in the middle of planning a solution to this problem.

Let's you and I make an effort or at least a plan to reduce or entirely stop eating at our desks.

Advanced: recall the stationary bike on which you can work, which is also a standing desk. Its surface is smaller than a regular desk which means there is no room for food on its surface. If you get a bike like that, it will immediately help you exercise more and eat less. Plus, if you are a klutz at assembly like I am, think of all the extra burned calories you will burn putting the bike together after it arrives.

CHAPTER 8:
TIME MANAGEMENT

1. Chapter introduction

Does this chapter even need an introduction? To manage your time better:

1) Prioritize tasks that will have the highest potential of getting you closer to your goals.
2) Have the discipline to take out low priority tasks.
3) Have more time left to do other important things.
4) Don't squander newly discovered extra time on frivolous things like watching TV.
5) Get important things accomplished.
6) Move your life and business forward.
7) You are happy. I am happy. You do more good things. The world becomes a better place, and in the midst of this euphoria you leave an amazing review about this book on Amazon.

It's that easy! Let's get started.

2. What, to you, constitutes time well spent?

Pardon me, I just realized that I've been a little rude. It was for your sake, of course, but still a bit rude. I've been projecting what I believe is time well spent for you and assuming that I had it right, all the while neglecting to ask what "time well spent" means for YOU.

If the idea of time well spent for you is hanging out with friends or being on vacation, then congratulations, you are normal. But for your work's sake, snap out of it immediately. Since this book is about business and professional productivity, I'd love it if time well spent for you, at least in large part, meant time spent working on your most important business or professional tasks. Ideally, you are working on something you are passionate about, and it is, therefore, time well spent.

Am I being a total hardline jerk? Let's establish some balance. Write down five things that constitute time well spent for you, with at least 2 of them being work-related. Feel welcome to include more work-related things in your list. If you are serious about being a successful entrepreneur or professional, I hope that working on your business constitutes time well spent for you. If not, we might have a disconnect with reality, wouldn't we?

After you've written down your 5, indicate next to each how often you get to do that particular thing.

Finally, look at your list and note the items you don't get to do enough of. Take some time to dive into each of the noted items by jotting down your responses to the following prompts.

- Why you don't get to do it?
- What distracted you from them?
- What gets in the way?
- Does something need to happen before you can do those things?
- What or who drains your time or energy, not letting you do the things you want to do?

If you can identify your biggest distractions, time-wasters, and energy drainers, you can begin taking steps to remove them from your life and replacing them with something more positive. Later in this chapter when we focus on scheduling. It will become apparent how easy it is to take out low-priority tasks that clutter your schedule and replace them with fewer tasks that are high-priority only.

3. Discipline: take nonessential tasks out of your schedule to make room for time well spent

Earlier in this book, we touched on taking out low priority tasks from your project list. Did you take them out?

You may have thought about it, and you may still be mulling it over. But without taking action, all this theory is useless. How about this time you take my advice and take nonessential tasks off your to-do list?

If you have not made your plan for today and for the week, and if you have not focused on taking low-priority tasks out of your schedule, picture me giving you a strict look with one eyebrow raised, and the other eyebrow lowered. That's my pretend angry look.

Now that I have you totally NOT intimidated, I'll ask nicely. Please, do the things suggested in this book.

We can pause here until you make a schedule for this week.

I'll assume that by this paragraph you made your schedule for the week. Now it is time to be a man (because if you are a woman you probably did better than the guys and already have an awesome daily and weekly schedule purged of non-essential tasks), and choose something to take out of your schedule.

I'll wait a few minutes for you to go through your weekly schedule or to-do list and take something out. If you already purged your list, try to take out another task. It doesn't have to be a big task. It can be something as small as a 30-minute task. You must get used to saying no to things.

You probably won't suffer from taking out your least important tasks, but you will immediately free up time to work on something that might make a big difference in your life. Doing this isn't easy at first, but if you stick with it, it will become natural. It is the simplest way to uncover the extra time in your life that you didn't think you had.

4. Case study: results after not answering phone/email/messages

Earlier in this book, we touched on not allowing distractions to creep in and ruin your focus. I want to give this more attention by sharing a personal case study.

I used to have a few people who would chat with me on Facebook chat or through phone text throughout the day. They would message me randomly whenever they wanted. I am sure you have people in your life who do that to you. Some of the messages I used to get were work-related, and some were not.

Through the process of researching and writing this book I also took a magnifying glass to my own habits. Responding to external communication was one area I really needed to focus on. I followed my own advice (how novel) and began waiting to reply to the messages I randomly get until a time that is convenient for me instead of jumping to reply.

In the past, after seeing a message, I would compulsively jump to reply to it. I felt like I was being rude if I didn't immediately answer. I had to train my mind not to jump to reply. Now I simply close the message or quickly reply to let the person know that I am busy and will answer later. When I do respond, it's during time I have designated for that purpose. This structure keeps my interruptions to a minimum.

Over time, this "trained" people not to randomly bother me during the workday with nonsense or fluff whenever they needed a break. I started getting more done, and people began to respect my time after I showed them that I respected it.

5. Benefits and tips for creating a weekly schedule/calendar

We've touched on the importance of keeping a calendar in

earlier chapters. I also suggested the Google Calendar mobile app for it. You can also maintain a Google Calendar on your computer.

In this section, let's create your weekly and daily schedule. If you work from your calendar, you won't let things creep in and distract you.

A good schedule is created ahead of time. Plan your week before it starts, and plan each day before that day starts. This way, when your weeks and days start, you will have laser focus, work on highest priority tasks and ignore low priority tasks.

Another benefit of keeping a schedule is that by virtue of being planned ahead of time, it isn't haphazardly put together. It is well thought out. If you let your time be spent on random tasks that pull you in different directions as your week goes by, there will be a higher chance of making poor time management decisions, which will lead to you wondering why you don't feel like you got much done at the end of your day or week.

Planning things ahead of time and sticking to them will also help you alleviate stress. As you become better at maintaining your schedule, you will learn to make enough time for the highest priority tasks, not procrastinate on them, and naturally get your most important tasks done without stressing out about it.

6. Schedule example

Your schedule becomes very easy to keep track of and maintain if you are good about taking out low-priority tasks and focusing on important tasks for long periods of time. In this section I'll show you an example of how I perfected this in my business.

First, I'll tell you a little bit about my business to give you an understanding of what I do. After that, I'll share the tasks that need to be done in my business. Then, I'll show you how I focus, prioritize, plan, schedule and manage my time.

A little bit about my business: my website is Problemio.com and my business is a collection of tools, mobile apps, books, courses, coaching, and some public speaking. These products and services aid entrepreneurs in planning, starting and growing their businesses.

Disclaimer: I am NOT sharing this to promote my business. I am sharing this to help you understand this case study example.

Here are all the tasks I can potentially be doing for my business at any given time:

- Writing books
- Supporting my paying customers
- Promoting my books
- Promoting my courses
- Promoting my coaching services
- Doing SEO (search enging optimization) for my website
- Doing social media marketing

- Updating my previous books
- Filming new courses
- Updating my older courses
- Creating YouTube videos
- Improving my apps

This list can keep going for a few more pages, but I'll spare you.

To give you a sense of the scope of total work that has to be done:

- I need to maintain and improve approximately 150 of my products which include apps, books and online courses.
- I need to keep making new and better products like this book.
- I need to promote all my existing 150+ products.
- I need to promote 1,000+ pieces of my content ranging from blog posts to YouTube videos.
- I need to devote time to helping my coaching clients.
- I need to devote time to do customer support.

I can't possibly do all this without prioritizing some things over others, and putting some tasks on hold for the sake of giving my best attention to a select few. You have to evaluate how much resources (time and money) you are able to allocate to projects and prioritize the highest potential tasks that can be successfully completed with the allocated resources.

Even though it would be ideal to give attention to everything, no company has unlimited resources to do that, and even the biggest companies have to prioritize. Luckily, the things you put off don't implode. Most of the time, they just sit there, waiting for you to eventually get to them. If they do need immediate attention, you can prioritize putting out immediate fires and emergencies, and when most of your business is on cruise control, it will be even easier to prioritize the most important tasks since nothing will be an emergency. Plus, as you run your business and work to automate or optimize regular tasks to be more efficient, it will help to not have to give them immediate attention.

Let me share how I prioritize.

1) Supporting current paying customers is the top priority
2) Promoting and growing my business
3) Improving current products
4) Creating new products

All these items are linked. I'll explain how shortly.

Each day, I allocate time to supporting existing customers. Making customers happy is the right thing to do in itself, but it is a fantastic marketing strategy because happy customers share their experiences with friends, leave nice reviews, and come back to buy more products from you. Supporting customers also informs me of what isn't perfect about my current products. I use that information to either improve my current products or create new ones. Over time I've become known for my genuine care and good customer support. As you can see, the first item on the list above feeds the second, third and fourth items, fueling everything in my business. A large part of my success has been due to my customer care. I prioritize this over almost anything, and other than family, it is the only thing I allow to break my focus during the day.

I am not saying that this should be the case for other businesses, but this has been one of the strongest engines of growth for my business, and it is my top priority.

When I am not supporting my customers, I follow an annual plan that I create for myself. That plan is broken down into months, weeks and days. At the end of each year, I make a general plan for the following year. This annual plan acts like a North Star that helps me stay focused on where I want my life and my business to be at the end of the year. At the end of each month that year, I make a general plan for the next month. At the end of each week, I make an outline and task plan for next week, and at the end of each day, I make a specific plan for the next day.

Now that you understand my business and what I am working on, I'll explain how I prioritized my current month, week and day.

This month, my goals are to:

1) Support my customers (which is also a marketing strategy)
2) Finish this book
3) Improve 5 of my existing online courses
4) Improve my Twitter marketing
5) Do SEO (search engine optimization) marketing for my website
6) If I complete items one through five on this list, I'll be able to start working on my projects for next month which include working on a new course or updating one of my older books

From that monthly plan, my plan this week is dominated by only two things:

1) Supporting my customers (this is always #1)
2) Writing this book whenever I am not with customers

I hope this illustrates the importance of prioritization. Out of the 1000+ tasks and 100+ products I could be working on, I prioritized only a few for an entire month. Prioritizing this way takes discipline. But once you do it, it allows you to devote enough time to your most important and mission-critical tasks.

After prioritizing, It is easy for me to plan my days because this week I have only two major things to focus on. Giving enough focus to writing will be the fastest way for me to finish this book. After that, I'll be able to move on to working on my next highest priority tasks.

Here is my schedule for today:

8am - 11am: Writing

11am - noon: Customer support

Noon - 2pm: Travel to the gym + gym + shower

2pm - 6pm: Writing

6pm - 7pm: Customer support

7:00pm: Done for the day.

If you prioritize correctly and plan ahead, time management is extremely easy.

7. Time management checklist

Here is a checklist to help you get organized when planning your schedule.

- Take out tasks that are not directly tied to your goals
- Allocate large blocks of time for focus on most important tasks, preferably one task at a time
- Plan months, weeks and days in advance

Time management can be simple if you plan ahead and exercise discipline in identifying high priority, goal-aligned tasks and take out low-priority tasks.

If you are a new or first-time entrepreneur, I realize that it is difficult to know which tasks to leave out and which to keep because they might all seem worthwhile for various reasons. Knowing which tasks will be more fruitful and have more potential takes experience. As one of the free extra resources I provide at the end of the book, you are welcome to email me personally with questions regarding your business and what to prioritize. I'll do my best to help you figure out priorities for your business and your tasks.

My personal email is:

alex.genadinik@gmail.com

I look forward to helping you.

CHAPTER 9:
BOOSTING YOUR MEMORY AND COGNITIVE ABILITY

1. Memory basics

Memory is a very underestimated part of productivity. Memory is tied to our physical and mental capacity to perform at a high level. By the end of this chapter, you will have a completely new understanding of where a large part of intelligence comes from, and how memory ties into your overall productivity and intelligence.

Improving your memory will help you learn new things faster and be more organized throughout your day. It will have far-reaching positive effects on many aspects of your life.

First, let's go over a few definitions.

Short-term memory - when our senses are hit with countless stimuli every second, there is a part of the brain where new information is stored for roughly 7 seconds. To retain anything longer, it must be focused on and stored in long-term memory. Short-term memory gets worse with age. You can improve it by playing mind games that force you to retain information. Short-term memory only temporarily holds information but does not actually store it.

Working memory - the brain's system for temporarily holding and processing information. The few items we focus on from our short-term memory have a chance to get into our long-term memory if we focus on them well enough while they are in our working memory. One unofficial way to think about this working memory is our consciousness. This is where we carry out complex tasks such as reasoning, learning, and comprehension. Our working memory can hold items for approximately 30 seconds. Working memory is highly correlated to fluid intelligence because the longer you can think about something and the more things you can think about during those 30 seconds, the better your reasoning will be. Whatever you are currently thinking about, that's your working memory at work.

Long-term memory - brain's system for long-term storage of information. Once a memory is stored as a long-term memory, you can recall it for years or decades after, depending on how strongly you associate that memory to other memories you have. Long-term health and wellness can boost your long-term memory. The use of mnemonics and memory tricks can help you retrieve items from your long-term memory. There are two types of long-term memory. The first type of long-term memory is Implicit long-term memory. It helps you with skills and remembering how to do things. The second type of long-term memory is explicit long-term memory. It deals with knowing things and information.

The two main takeaways I'd like you to focus on are:

1) You have a much higher chance to remember something long-term if you focus on it with your working memory.
2) Working memory capacity is highly correlated to intelligence. It is important to train it to make it better.

Many people think that they forget things like names, facts or numbers because they have a bad memory. But for many people, the problem is that they never knew that information in the first place. If the information just gets to your short-term memory but doesn't get processed and retained, you never really knew it. The differentiator is to focus on whatever you need to remember with your working memory. That will give you a greater chance of remembering information and retrieve it from your long-term memory later.

Now that you understand the importance of focus when it comes to retaining new important information, I'll give you a few mental tricks to make sure you never forget anything important.

Here is a small trick to remember things. This trick helps you focus on whatever information you need to retain. The focusing process will help your brain do something scientists call "encoding." The trick is called "Focus and Picture." I learned it from Barry Reitman who regularly consults with the New York Police Department to help officers improve their memory. When you need to remember something, relate it to something in a silly, whacky, incongruous relationship and then picture those two things together. It will be unique and shocking enough to increase the chances of the new information getting enough focus to get stored in your long-term memory.

Once the information is focused on and encoded, the brain goes through a process of consolidation which is like gluing the memory together to other associations and naturopaths needed for retrieval. Lastly, the memory can only be called a memory after it has been recalled. The process of recalling a memory is called retrieval.

When you need to remember a certain fact, in your mind's eye, put whatever you need to remember next to a pre-chosen item. Make the combination whacky. Like a cat singing opera or a house inside a microwave to help you make the memory a little shocking to help it stand out.

Another trick I learned from Barry is for how to never forget something at home when you are heading out. Barry suggests making a list of items you need to take with you, and taping a piece of paper with that list next to your door. You won't miss it when you head out.

2. How to boost your memory and keep it functioning well

There are a number of things you can do to improve your memory. Some of these things are common sense. Here are some examples:

1) Eating a healthy diet full of fruits and vegetables instead of processed foods filled with sugar
2) Get regular exercise and maintain your overall health
3) Take supplements that help with brain function

4) Get plenty of sleep
5) Get mental stimulation rather than doing mindless activities like watching TV
6) Reduce stress which kills brain cells
7) Protect your brain from too many distractions
8) Read more books
9) Play thinking games like chess

Some exercises to improve working memory are:

1) Rehearsal and repetition
2) Chunking or breaking down large pieces of information into smaller ones
3) Pairing mental images with clues that help you store and retrieve information from long-term memory
4) Mnemonics

CHAPTER 10:
EFFICIENCY AND PROCESS OPTIMIZATION

1. Chapter introduction

Increasing efficiency has to do with:

- Outsourcing
- Delegating
- Automating
- Optimizing processes
- Intelligently planning ahead to choose the most efficient strategy rather than trying to figure it out on the spot
- Improving the strength and quality of your immediate focus

We've covered quite a bit of theory in this book so I'd like to turn now to focus on practical examples. In this section, I'll walk you through some common tasks and processes that a modern business might need, and show you how each of those can be more efficient.

2. Automation and optimization philosophy for business

It is critical that you set up your businesses and marketing activities in such a way that the majority of tasks can be automated over time. Maximizing automation opportunities in your business allows you to devote additional resources to your most important tasks rather than the minutiae.

In fact, automation is one of the first strategies that cross my mind during the business planning phases of a new marketing strategy, business strategy or a business idea. I need to know how to correctly position that business in order to automate most of it so a large part of it can eventually run on cruise control so that I can devote scarce resources and attention to its most important aspects.

Many online business ideas can be almost entirely automated. If you have a book on Amazon, a course on Udemy, or if you are selling a product from your own website, if you set up your marketing to be fully automated, you can get sales regularly, and put your attention elsewhere like building new marketing channels, improving your current product offerings or making new products.

When evaluating a new business idea or a strategy, immediately run through these items:

- Identify the primary components of the project
- For each component, consider what can be automated, optimized or outsourced
- Estimate the project's highest and realistic potential
- Add together the resources (time and money required)

146

needed to implement the project, optimization, outsourcing, automation, man-hours
- Decide whether the potential reward is worth the resources

If the potential of the project exceeds the resources it requires, you can proceed. If not, re-strategize the project or reject it. Proper application of efficiency techniques within a project plan can sometimes make a project feasible by making it less resource intensive and less risky to implement.

3. Efficiency tips for how I wrote 14 books in 55 days which allowed for rapid market testing

This book is my 21st. I'll be the first to admit that not all of them are good. I'll also be the first to point out which books I am most proud of, and which are even used at some major universities.

It took me a long time to improve my writing and become better at promoting my books. Success with books was not quick for me. It took years of struggle before any of my books did well. One day I decided that I needed more and better books on Amazon to become successful there. After a brainstorming session with myself and a big whiteboard (lots of arrows), I came up with 18 books that I felt had a niche market to them, and that I had a chance to write the best book in each niche market.

The problem was precisely that I wanted to write 18 books, which for some people would take years, and I could not take that much time away from my main business. I created an aggressive and efficient writing plan. I gave myself two months during which I planned to produce 18 quality books, with some of the shorter books having as little as two days allocated to their writing and editing. I had to make every part of my book creation as efficient as possible.

Here are the productivity strategies I used:

- I extended my workdays and <u>focused</u> only on writing during those days. This gave me <u>large blocks of time in which to focus on only one thing.</u> The stronger focus immediately made me a more efficient writer, and I was able to fly through the books.

- I got <u>daily exercise and sleep</u> which helped me maintain a strong focus and keep up my enthusiasm throughout the day as I was writing.

- <u>I eliminated distractions</u> and <u>cleared other projects off my plate</u> before I began this writing "sprint."

- I wrote the first drafts of the books as quickly as possible. It was okay if there were mistakes because those mistakes were going to be fixed during the editing.

- I <u>planned</u> the books in a way that some of the chapters could be <u>reused</u> in multiple books. Since all the books were on different business and marketing topics, there was some overlap. For example, a chapter on business card marketing was reused in three books.

- The lengths of the books were condensed to only have the bare essentials needed to get published. My plan was to see which books had promising sales after being published, and later improve those books in their second and third editions.

Every day was a sprint of focused writing. In the end, I exhausted myself after writing 14 books within 55 days, and simply could not force myself to write any longer. I needed a break. Luckily, I had already written my highest priority books and was fine with leaving out the low priority ones.

The rapid writing and immediate self-publishing of the books on Amazon allowed me to quickly market-test the books. When I created my initial plan for the 14 books, that plan was based on a few years of experience of being a writer. Even with the experience of being a self-published author, it was difficult to predict whether the books would sell once they were published. I had to move from theory by making the books live in the market in order to test my hypothesis about which of the books would sell well.

From the 14 books I wrote, only 3 went on to sell well. If I had written just one or two books, those would have likely been duds, and I would have concluded that I was a failure, and quit. Instead, my efficient approach enabled a big market test that gave me real-world data regarding which books would succeed. After that test, I went on to write second editions for the books that showed signs of life and made them the best books in their respective niches.

Main takeaway:

Efficiency allows rapid prototyping of ideas and rapid practical market tests of those ideas

4. Efficiency and optimization tips for automating your marketing

Between my books, online courses, mobile apps, coaching services, and even some B2B offerings, I have about 200 products that I promote on a daily basis.

I can only give my focus to promoting a handful of those products at a time. So how can I possibly promote all of them well?

During the planning phase of any business or a new product, before any work has been done, make sure that there are natural marketing strategies available that will allow you to promote the new business/product in a hands-off way. For my business, I made it easy for people to find my products by making sure that the products were well-positioned in SEO so that when potential clients are searching for help in certain areas, they discover my products. That allowed me to be hands-off, sometimes only learning about the new clients after seeing money deposited in my bank account.

You might think that a hands-off strategy is unique to online businesses, but this is an equally common marketing strategy for traditional offline businesses. There are two ways that traditional offline businesses can (and should) leverage user discovery in order to get new clients:

1) Optimized location - opening a business that has a storefront on a busy street where there are many people passing by and discovering the business every day.
2) Optimized web presence - creating a website that ranks

highly in Google search, leveraging business listing websites like Yelp, Google Local, Yellow Pages, and similar websites.

You might ask what happens when a business doesn't have natural marketing paths for user discovery. That isn't uncommon. Some businesses have more natural ways in which they can be effectively promoted than others. My answer is that during the business planning phase, evaluate the resources needed to promote your business. If you can't automate the marketing in a big way, and can't get viral sharing, it is a warning sign that too many resources would have to be allocated to marketing. Unless the potential of the business is immense, I would warn against moving ahead because businesses that can't be promoted efficiently have an extra layer of risk.

Main takeaway:

Plan for marketing efficiency before even getting into a business.

5. How to optimize the use of video, audio and written content creation

You can create a significant amount of quality content in less time than you think. Here are a few simple strategies for content reuse and repurposing to maximize your content creation and quality.

Here are the most common forms of content media:

- Video on YouTube

- Video on premium online courses
- Audio on iTunes podcasts and other podcasting websites
- Text in a book
- Text on your blog

Video content is the most versatile form of content. It contains audio and can be transcribed into written content.

You can start by making a very long and comprehensive YouTube video. That is the first product. This video can be extrapolated and reworked to make many additional products, each in less time than you would think since you would be working with a base of that product already completed.

Here is an example of what I mean:

1) You can take the audio from the YouTube video and turn it into a podcast episode.
2) You can transcribe the video yourself or outsource transcription, and turn the text into a blog post.
3) You can extrapolate on your original topic and turn it into a video series with examples and a few extra resources, and turn it into a YouTube series instead of just one YouTube video.
4) You can turn the video series into a premium video-based online course.
5) You can transcribe each of the lectures in the course, and turn each lecture into a blog post and a podcast episode.
6) You can turn all those blog posts into a book.
7) You can offer one on one coaching on the topic of your course and book.
8) You can make apps or software tools around the same

subject matter.

The best part of all this is that the time and money you save through so much content reuse and repurposing, and the greater potential you give yourself on all these additional websites and platforms allows you to spend more time, money and effort perfecting and promoting your content, which gives you another natural long-term advantage.

You can take this to another level by publishing all these products on multiple platforms per product type. For example, apps can be on Android, iPhone and even Amazon. Books can be sold on Amazon, Barnes & Noble and many other websites. Courses can be sold on Udemy and Skill-share, and so on.

Despite starting with an idea for one piece of content, you can immediately have a presence on 20 large online websites and platforms. Win!

6. How to efficiently set up your environment for video and audio production

Many people geek out about high end cameras, lighting equipment, and microphones which produce professional-quality video and audio, but to efficiently start recording video and audio content in your office, you often need just the bare minimum equipment.

If you want to record audio and video content as early as to-day, all you need is the right software, the right kind of lighting and background, and to choose the right kind of content you will create.

Obviously, if you want to create action movies, you will need to invest more time and money into getting high end equipment and maybe even hiring people to help you. But you don't need that for many types of online content. You can often get away with just having the following:

- Free screencast software that came with your computer or software like ScreenFlow or Camtasia which will record screencasts or HD video of you by using your computer's built-in camera. That saves you money and time on not having to buy a camera. This kind of software usually costs around $99 or less if you can get it on sale.

- Lighting for recording. This can be bought for under $100, and if your recording area is bright enough from natural light, you may not need to invest in the lighting equipment.

- If you can record in a quiet area, you may get away with using the built-in microphone of your laptop, which would save you from having to buy an external microphone.

- You can create a simple and elegant background at home or office or simply buy a green screen and a stand for under $100.

And voila, you are ready to record.

7. Learning new skills

As a professional, you must be able to learn new skills quickly. If you don't, the world will pass you by. I'll use an example of learning to code since that is such a popular and difficult thing to learn in today's world. You should be able to use these strategies to learn and apply new skills quickly.

The best and fastest learning happens when you use all of these strategies together:

- Read and watch free tutorials online
- Read books
- Take video-based online courses
- Hire coaches and mentors
- Use online forums and communities to get help when you are stuck or confused
- Apply the skills you learned, and learn by doing

When I was creating my mobile apps, I started by going through free online tutorials. When I got stuck, which was often, I would use a website like stackoverflow.com which is a community of software developers that help each other. I also grew my knowledge by taking online courses, and hiring freelancers to coach me through difficult parts of app development rather than having them write all the code for me. I was also practicing the skills I was learning, making my own software engineering skills better.

Some people are prone to thinking that they need to go back to college to get an engineering degree or certificate, but if you are resourceful in how you approach learning, you can learn most skills on your own faster, cheaper and arguably better than you would in college.

The takeaway:

Be resourceful about leveraging learning materials, community help, and coaching to help you build skills faster and more effectively than you would by using one learning resource or strategy at a time.

8. Project planning to be efficient and organized with outlines

Before starting on any project, create a plan of action and a thorough outline for it. Once you have an outline in place, it will help you speed through the project because it is organized and you know what to do at each step.

For an example of an outline, look at the table of contents of this book. I made the table of contents first. After I planned the table of contents, I had 90% of the book structure in place and it was easy to write each section one by one without getting off track.

9. What not to make efficient or optimized

There are some parts of your business that will require your deepest love and care. Usually, those parts of the business are:

- Customer care
- Making customers happy
- Understanding the needs of your customers
- Going the extra mile for your clients and overdelivering
- Taking time to understand how your customers are currently using your product, and how to make your product even better for them

You understand where I am going with this, right? Not only is making your customers happy the right thing to do, but happy customers can turn into people who return to buy more from you later, leave nice online reviews about your business, and recommend your business to their friends. You must create an army of happy and loyal (as loyal as possible in today's world) customers.

10. My optimization and efficiency strategy of fitting tasks into "time-spaces"

I played a lot of chess growing up (feel welcome to challenge me to an online game on chess.com - my screen name there is genadinik. If you beat me, you get a prize), and sometimes I think that playing chess from an early age wired my brain for consistently trying to work on some strategy.

As you can probably relate, there are a million things to do each day. Some of my daily tasks include tech support, answering email and messages from clients, friends and employees, checking various analytics, creating new products, promoting products, and a million other small tasks that pop up each day. I don't have time to do all that, but I find "nooks and crannies" of time in which I can fit tasks.

Even if you are awesome and keep a detailed daily and weekly calendar, you might find that each day there are many separate bits of free time that occur between larger tasks you have planned.

Some examples of such bits of time include:

- Wating for someone or something else or in line at a store
- Sitting in public transportation, cabs, planes
- Walking somewhere

These moments can occur spontaneously or as a part of our schedules, and can take 1, 3, 5, 10, 15, 30 or 60+ minutes. Be aware of all the small tasks you need to do in your day, and plan ahead for doing appropriate tasks when a chunk of time that opens up within your day.

For example, if I am walking to the grocery store, I have 5 minutes to answer short messages or email. I know this is not the safest thing I can do, but all of us have been guilty of this at one time or another. If my mother is reading this and worrying that I will get run over while answering email on my phone while crossing the street, don't worry mom, I never do this. Wink. This can also be done through a voice dictation app which would make answering email while walking much safer and faster. When I get to the store and have to wait in line, I might answer short messages. When I am on public transportation for 15 minutes or longer, I use my smartphone to write blog posts or parts of my books. In fact, 50% of the first draft of this book was written using my smartphone while I was riding the New York City subway. Another 15% of the first draft of this book was written on long plane rides, and the rest of the first draft was written while pedaling on a stationary bike at the gym. The trick was to keep matching the amount of available time to what I could accomplish during that time. If I had a 20-minute subway ride or a 30-minute stationary bike ride, I'd just type away on my phone during those times, and when the time was up, I would sometimes have a few hundred words written. Over time that added up to a 200+ page book which is over 50,000 words.

Aha moment:

This book is over 200 pages, but its first draft took <u>zero actual workdays</u> to write because I wrote it during otherwise "wasted" time like the commute, plane rides, or biking at the gym.

Another person might have taken a month or two of full-time work to write a draft of a 200 page book. I am not bragging. I am simply illustrating the power of reclaiming "wasted" time.

Of course, the editing of this book had to be done more carefully since writing on the plane or public transportation introduces more errors and typos, but I got it done without diverting time or resources from my main business.

11. Multitasking and efficiency

Many people think that multitasking is a good way to be more efficient. In reality, people can only focus on one thing at a time. If you are doing more than one thing at a time, you are just quickly shifting your focus from one task to another, but never able to give attention to more than one task.

Multitasking diverts your attention, dilutes your focus, decreases your attention to detail and causes you to make more mistakes in your work. If you multitask and make more errors than usual, fixing those errors will waste the time you thought you saved, and then some. Plus, if errors creep into the final product, it might create dissatisfied customers.

12.Don't work while tired, and know when to rest

Working while tired or when you are not 100% causes inefficiency. If you are starting a business or doing professional work, you need your focus to be as sharp as possible, and you need attention to detail.

If you work while tired or not fully alert, you will be much more likely to make many more mistakes just like you would if you were distracted. You might create errors that may take hours to hunt down and fix.

Plus, when you are tired, you work more slowly and the work is less enjoyable and feels more like drudgery. If you need to, and are able to, make it a point to get enough rest to feel alert when working. When you get back to feeling rested and alert, you will naturally work better and faster, and you will accomplish much more in less time.

13.Making communication more efficient

In a typical work environment, we often communicate with employees, business partners, and customers through email and text chat. When email and text chat require many messages sent back and forth, they become extremely inefficient because you are either sitting around and waiting for a response or getting distracted from your work each time you get a new chat message.

Whenever possible, use these communication tactics to make your communication more efficient:

- Communicate via chat or email during your "nook and

cranny" time when you have a few free seconds or minutes, instead of allowing email or text messages to distract you from your current task.

- If you need to discuss things in detail, offer to call the person on the phone or via Skype which uses video to make the conversation more personable and efficient. Video calls are usually better than just phone because there are less misunderstandings since you can see the person's body language and facial expressions.
- Offer to meet and chat in person if they are in the same office.
- Set a deadline to resolve the communication. The deadline can be artificial, like saying that you have a meeting in 5 minutes when you might not. A deadline can make the conversation more focused and less meandering. Extra urgency will sometimes get the person you are communicating with to get to their points faster and go on less tangents.

PART 2:

THE BIGGER PICTURE

CHAPTER 11:
MINDFULNESS AND SELF-AWARENESS

1. Chapter introduction: philosophy

If nothing else, my overuse of the word philosophy throughout this book is pissing off Plato in heaven (or as he would say I am pissing off his soul that lived after his physical body died). Sorry Plato, but I am about to drop some more pseudo-philosophy.

Self-awareness is an extremely important and underrated topic in productivity. If you are not in touch with yourself, you will be prone to mistakes when choosing your professional and life goals which will lead to natural mistakes in choosing what to work on. When you choose the wrong things to work on, all that work will be largely for nothing. In this chapter I'll focus on making you more self-aware with the goal of empowering you to make better decisions for how to better direct your life, and with that, your projects.

As citizens of the modern world, you and I are responsible for figuring out what to do with our lives. We are responsible for our choice if we get it right, and we have to live with our choice if we make a mistake.

Only a few hundred years ago, most people would answer the question of "what should I do with my life and what will fulfill me?" with religious teachings. Then a pesky philosophical movement came along called Existentialism. Plato, this one isn't my fault.

Existentialism is a movement that largely rejected God and organized religion. For the first time in the history of philosophy, mass culture, and rational thought, Existentialism put the burden of deciding what a person should do with their life squarely on their shoulders.

Soren Kierkegaard is considered to be the father of Existentialism. He lived in the mid-1800s. Shortly after him, Friedrich Nietzsche took the Existentialist baton, and wrote his famous quote, "God is dead, and man killed him." With that quote, modern thinkers, followed by the rest of society, began to give God less importance, and more importance to rational thought.

Throughout the following 100 years, additional prominent philosophers insisted that we get to know ourselves as deeply as possible because that's the only way to accurately decide for ourselves what each of us is meant to do with our life - a deeply personal decision.

It might also be worth noting that the world also witnessed two horrific world wars, and began to question how man was able to create so much evil when given full control over his destiny. A part of the answer became another philosophical movement called Nihilism.

Nihilism sounds depressing at first, but its proponents claim that the negativity is only on the surface, and that Nihilism is actually positive. See for yourself. Nihilism rejects the idea of God and afterlife. According to Nihilism, we should make peace with the idea that regardless of how much importance we attribute to ourselves, each of us is a tiny, irrelevant speck in a big universe that does not care about us. Our impact on the word is also negligible to the universe. For the most part, other than our legacy or anything we made that remained after us, our impact on the world ends when our life ends.

According to Nihilism, things to which we attribute importance, only matter to us. We attribute meaning to things in our minds. But that is only in our minds. Nothing matters to the cold and dark universe. It will keep spinning with or without us.

This is the part of Nihilism that people say sounds depressing. But isn't it also freeing? If the universe doesn't care, we can do what we want. Our mistakes and failures in life aren't as costly as we make them out to be. We can take unnecessary pressure off our shoulders, and choose to do what is important to us and what makes us happy. According to Nihilism, our responsibility is first and foremost to ourselves because there is no life after death, and if we get it wrong during our life, there are no takebacks.

This is why we have to get to know ourselves as well as possible to make sure that the choices we make us happy in the end. That's why self-awareness and mindfulness are so important. They help us get to know ourselves. The better we know ourselves, the better decisions we will make when deciding what to do with our lives, and that will help us correctly choose what to work on professionally, and how to lead our lives.

If you choose the right projects to work on, you will be infinitely more productive than if you choose mistaken goals and projects or projects someone else chooses for you. Let's help ourselves by practicing mindfulness and self-awareness, increasing the chance of choosing the right direction for our lives.

Now that I illustrated the importance of self-awareness, I'll give you the bad news. There is an assault on our self-awareness from two sources:

1) Our own psychological defense mechanisms.
2) Our external environment and modern culture which are increasingly shaped by large institutions, companies, and organizations that endlessly compete for our attention, distract us from turning inward and don't have our best interest in mind. Companies and institutions do anything they can to get you to grab your attention and shape your perception of the world into one that is most conducive for them to make more money or impose their will on the world.

2. Psychological defense mechanisms

As you tippytoe, quietly opening a door to a dark room, a monster jumps at you with a soul wrenching shriek as you slam the door shut. Better not look again if you don't have to, right? Better keep that door closed.

This is how some of your psychological defense mechanisms work. They seek pleasure and avoid pain.

While some people look inside themselves with curiosity, many others find looking inside themselves unpleasant, and painful, especially if they discover something in their subconscious that they don't like. You can't hide from yourself once you find something you don't like about yourself.

You might be thinking that instead of having that reaction, many people can just fix whatever negative aspect of themselves they discovered. To that I would say:

1) People who are able to do that are the people already looking inside themselves with curiosity. They are not as afraid.
2) Many people don't have such a healthy approach to things.
3) Even when people fix whatever they didn't like about themselves, it is still an experience filled with enough difficult emotions that make many people wary about looking inside again.

You have to be curious and brave to look inside. Over time, one of two things will happen. Either you will get comfortable turning inward, become your own best friend, and laugh with yourself at your own imperfections and humanity, or you will be increasingly scared to look inside, which will require more and more courage each time until you eventually stop looking inward, or do an arguably bigger disservice to yourself, which is convincing yourself that you are still a brave person not afraid to look inside, simply not finding the right time to do so when really living the life of a coward.

That was the psychological defense problem. But there is an even bigger problem - our environment.

3. Culture and external environment

We are living in an "experimental culture" and "experimental environment" which is changing and evolving at a rate that the world has never seen before.

Here are a few factors that are new, which as individuals we don't quite know how to deal with:

1) For the last few decades we have been increasingly subjected to an enormous amount of direct and subconscious advertisements. Each of them impacts our desires, emotions, fears, and world views in a way that the advertiser needs in order for them to sell more of their products to us, or have us do something else that is beneficial to them.

2) We are increasingly addicted to screens of all shapes and sizes like TV, computers and smartphones. The companies we interact with through those screens are experts at addicting us to their content and turning us into zombies that do what they need us to do.

Have you ever had an experience with your phone where you take it out to check the time or another trivial thing, get distracted by some alert, tend to that alerts, put the phone away, and realize that you didn't actually check the time or whatever you wanted to check when you took out your phone?

This happens to me every once in a while, and it happens to many people I've asked. This is an example of how effective companies have become at getting our attention and diverting it from our initial intentions.

3) There are more and more companies vying for our attention. Their survival depends on whether they are able to get our attention. If they capture our attention, they can make us buy their products and money from us. If they don't capture our attention, they don't get us to see or use their products, become irrelevant, don't make money from us, and ultimately die.

4) We are increasingly connected to companies, institutions, information and devices, but less to people.

5) Companies and other organizations have an agenda for us that isn't necessarily our best interest. I would say it rarely coincides with our best interest even if it starts out well-intentioned.

6) Companies and organizations communicate to us through a safe, widely accepted, narrow set of politically correct concepts. They can't do anything politically incorrect even if it is the right thing to do because companies and institutions must avoid controversy and backlash that could lead to them losing customers, sources of funding or revenue.

7) The most powerful companies have direct influence over government, education and law in order to make it easier for them to capture your attention, and get you to become a "happy," long-term customer.

8) 90% of all consumed media (music, TV, newspapers, radio, websites, etc) is owned by just a few very wealthy

individuals that are major shareholders in some of the biggest media companies in the world. They all know each other well, and are in constant dialog and "coopetition."

Here is an example. There are a handful of major record companies that own 90% of all consumed music in the United States. Whenever any independent musician becomes popular, they sign that musician. They decide which musicians get promoted, and which don't. To a large degree, they also approve or disapprove their message, brand, and a large part of the lyrics. It is a part of how they shape or curate our entire culture.

The same media companies also own TV, radio, and many websites so that they can strategically promote whichever artist, idea or cultural aspect they feel will be most beneficial to them.

Earlier in my career, I worked for a company that was bought by one of these media giants. I won't say their name so they don't come after me. I'll just say that it was one of the top media companies in the US. They own many TV channels, websites, and other types of mass media that you and I consume on a regular basis without realizing that they are all owned by one giant company. They are our source of news, entertainment and often education. They shape our world's culture and ideas in a big way.

As an employee, I was shocked when I learned that they developed programming internally, or bought out TV networks, websites, and other media according to the motto, "we get them from birth to death." I was shocked to see the level and organization of systematic brainwashing they were pushing into our culture and all of us unsuspecting citizens.

This is best illustrated by the fact that they owned one of the biggest TV channels for kids and one of the biggest TV channels for people over 65 years old. They also owned many channels aimed at all the demographics in between. By owning nearly all content you and I consume, these giant media companies "curate" us into becoming drone consumers that are ideal to these companies. Welcome to the matrix.

These companies literally "curate" us into whatever is most profitable for them. By curating each and every one of us, they curate our collective culture, which is the experimental culture inside which you and I live.

It's profitable for them to keep us intelligent enough to function and work in society in order to be able to make money to spend, but not smart enough to question this matrix too deeply, and remain happy consuming whatever they want us to consume from music to cars to food to television and movies to everything else in our lives they can control.

Ironically, it's not even their fault. You can trace back a major fault in the system that demands publicly traded companies to chase profits. A public company CEO's main job is to maximize shareholder profits, putting pressure on the CEO to find ways to generate as much revenue and profits for the company as possible. These companies might start out well-intentioned, just providing a nice service to us. But at some point, they all have to become well-oiled money-making machines that would trample over ethics if that is necessary for profit.

These large companies need us to consume and want things endlessly. In truth, most people don't need much for happiness. The things you and I need for happiness aren't material. They are things like fulfillment, freedom, inner calm, health and safety, creative and engaging work, healthy relationships, and family.

Unfortunately (given our current system), most of those things don't make much money for corporations. Instead of those things, they need us to think that the Marlboro man is cool, that we need to dress and live like celebrities, have the coolest car, go on the coolest vacations, and turn our lives into an endless pursuit of stuff. And if you think that this is a static situation, here comes more bad news. These companies are getting better and better at getting you to give them your attention regardless of where you are or what you are doing. If you aren't staring at a screen, you are getting hit with billboard ads, radio or their branding and logos on other people's stuff. When watching TV, you might think that the commercials are the things that appear every 15 minutes to break up the content, but you can just as easily look at almost all television programming as a promotion of lifestyle or imposition of our culture, what we like and what we don't.

Scary, but why is this relevant here? Besides me feeling like it was time for me to go on a tirade, it is relevant because these companies are diverting our attention from going inwards.

For your sake, you must work to reverse this trend and maintain enough self-awareness and mindfulness to fully understand yourself, stay out of the matrix, and make life decisions that will fulfill you in the right ways for you, rather than making life decisions that seem like they make sense, but are really mis-goals towards which you get pulled by people and companies vying for your attention and consumption.

Now that I've painted such a rosy picture, I should apologize for going so dark on you. My goal was to keep this book light and fun to read. Fail.

We do have hope. That hope is to make ourselves more self-aware. One way to become more self-aware is to practice Mindfulness.

4. Two Mindfulness definitions

There is a type of meditation called Mindfulness Meditation. After everything I've put you through in this book, I'll take it easy, and won't try to turn you into a yogi. Instead, I'll give you a pseudo goal to simply practice self-awareness.

Let me define the kind of self-awareness I have in mind. From now on, I'd like you to give more attention to your passing thoughts, and the different "train cars" in your trains of thought.

Practice tracing back passing thoughts to their roots. For example, if you are struggling with procrastination, try to trace back your train of thought to catch the thought that diverted you from starting, and caused you to get off track. Does it happen because of negative emotions? If you sense some negativity, focus on it a bit deeper. What precisely is the negative emotion? Is it a feeling of anxiety and being overwhelmed? Is it low confidence? Where is the feeling of being overwhelmed, low confidence or anxiety coming from? Is it from lack of experience or inability to overcome some challenging part within an overall project? Is it from self-doubt?

Once you dig far enough to uncover the root causes of what's holding you back, you can focus on overcoming those problems and move forward in your project or your life.

Sometimes you can trace thoughts and feelings with simple self-awareness and increased focus on what is happening inside your heart and mind. Sometimes you need more powerful tools. One of those tools is the actual regular practice of Mindfulness Meditation. Other tools are getting coaching from a life coach or a mental health professional.

Many thoughts and ideas we become aware of while practicing self-awareness or Mindfulness aren't written down on paper. They are often abstract. What's even worse is that it is difficult to tell if they indicate a need for change. The decisions presented to you by self-awareness discoveries are necessarily difficult. If they weren't difficult, you would have already noticed and fixed them, and they wouldn't be hiding in your subconscious, placed there by your psychological defenses.

After making a decision to change, many people still run into the problem of inaction because they fall back on existing behaviors that are comfortable and familiar.

Change in action only comes if you clearly decide that

change is necessary, and its impact is sorely needed because your current way of doing things is severely failing you. A good coach, therapist, or peer mastermind group can help you identify problem points faster, but only you can make the final decision that the change is necessary, and desire the change. Once you desire the change bad enough, that desire will be the inertia that will get you to take deliberate action.

5. Blaming and looking for scapegoats

At first glance, we can all think of friends that fall into the mental trap of making mistakes and immediately blaming other people or circumstances, but never themselves. You and I certainly don't do that, right? Wrong. We've all been guilty of this at one time or another.

When something doesn't go right, many of us do a quick mental scan of possible external causes for failure in search of where to place blame so that the blame doesn't have to be pointed at us. But wouldn't we learn more about how to improve what went wrong if we looked inward for what we could have done better?

If you train yourself to do that, and work on making yourself increasingly more self-aware of where you fall short in your business projects, work or personal life, you will be more likely to uncover weaknesses that can then be fixed.

We simply don't know what we don't know. As long as we don't know all the things that we could do better, we won't improve at those things. Allowing ourselves to realize what we don't do as well as we could, is the first step to improving.

6. Mindfulness exercise one

I hope you are not afraid to look inward because this exercise is all about leaving you alone with yourself, without any distractions.

Some people find the prospect of looking inwards to be depressing, while others (nerds like me) find self-discovery exhilarating. These two groups of people don't understand one another. People who like to look inside themselves never understand the people who find it depressing, and the depressed people don't understand the people who actually like to look inside themselves. It's like cats and dogs.

If you are in the camp of people who don't like spending time looking inwards, what I am about to suggest will be like trying to feed a small child food that they hate. But trust me, this spinach of life can be good for you, and we'll take baby steps. Please be open to trying this exercise. I'll start gently, just for you.

For your first exercise, all you have to do is go outside for a walk WITHOUT your phone or anyone else so that there are no distractions. Ideally, you would go for a walk in a park with greenery (potheads, by greenery I mean real grass and trees that are still alive, okay?). Nature helps our brains relax and it is conducive to creativity. If you don't have a park nearby, the next best thing is to go for a walk in a quiet and convenient area where you live.

All I ask is that you start with a 10 minute walk with no distractions. Seems easy, right? Good, because I would like you to take this walk every day for a month. The purpose of doing this for a month is to make it a habit, and to become comfortable doing it. You can add it to your daily schedule like you saw me allocate two hours for the gym when I shared my schedule.

When you walk, thoughts will begin to flow. Most of those thoughts will be uneventful, but some will be fascinating. Just get comfortable having them, and being in that mental space.

It will prepare you for your next exercise.

7. Exercise two

Once you've gotten into the habit of daily 10-minute walks, the next step is extending the duration of your walking sessions. As before, make sure you are walking in quiet (and safe) areas, ideally with lots of greenery. You should try to be in nature as much as possible.

For this exercise, build up your walking sessions to 30 or maybe even 60 minutes if you feel physically comfortable doing that. Walking is a wonderful exercise with many health benefits. It also lets your mind wander and relax.

Try this because you really won't like what I've cooked up for you in the next section.

8. Exercise three

In this exercise we'll try some simple meditation. This isn't necessary, but I'd like you to give it a fair try.

It is difficult to show meditation in a book. Plus, I am not a meditation teacher. You are better off searching YouTube for "Mindfulness Meditation." Many experienced practitioners will show you and guide you how to do it better than I can by written text.

Once you have a sense of the practice, try it a few times for 5-10 minutes each time and see how you feel. I realize that this may be too unusual for some people so I won't insist on it. Simply try it to see if you enjoy it. If not, just stick to the walking exercises.

I don't know about your productivity, but with the walking exercises, the stationary bike, and treadmill desks, I may just be training you for the next Olympics.

CHAPTER 12:
LIFE PURPOSE

1. What exactly is life purpose?

If you don't know what life purpose is, how can I explain it? It's just arguably the single most important thing for you to figure out. No pressure.

One of the best ways to discover your life purpose is to get to know yourself. That's why I started the second part of the book by suggesting that you practice self-awareness, mindfulness, and get comfortable looking inward. Looking inside yourself will help you discover your life purpose and the life goals that are ideal for *you*. Being more self-aware will also help you avoid the trap of following a life purpose that someone else or some organization has set for you.

Pause.

I have been getting a bit negative and dark. I know. "My bad" as the kids say. This book started out so lighthearted and fun, and now I've gone dark on you for two chapters in a row. I promise to reboot myself by the next chapter.

End pause.

Giving yourself a life purpose isn't a prerequisite for life. It is a prerequisite for a rich inner life, and days filled with purpose, meaning and fulfillment. If you don't have to have a life purpose, you can just float through life, and after a while you will die just like people with a life purpose do. The universe doesn't care with your life. It's up to you.

When presented with a choice of a meaningful life of purpose, and one without, most people choose door number one. You owe it to yourself to identify the life purpose that best fits your internal makeup, and who you truly are. Keep in mind that as you go through life, grow, gain new experiences, and change, your life purpose may change too. It doesn't have to be a static entity. You are a very different person at 20 years old than at 60. As long as you are in tune with yourself, you will get better at adjusting your life purpose according to what you need to feel fulfilled.

2. The mistake not to make when trying to figure out your life purpose

When people are asked what their life purpose is, most people admit that they have not identified it.

Of course, you are not like most people. You are awesome. You surely have your life purpose figured out. But what about all the people who don't?

There are three very distinct strategies through which to discover your life purpose.

1) Practicing Mindfulness and self-awareness.
2) Trying out different hobbies and interests, hoping that

one thing will lead to another, after which you will eventually stumble into your life purpose.

3) Going through life, waiting for more meaning, but not doing much about it, wondering why your life purpose doesn't come to you.

A combination of strategies one and two is an ideal approach to identify your life purpose. But few people do that. Most people sit around, waiting for their life purpose to pop into their heads, wondering why it doesn't. Waiting for it to simply come to you is a mistake.

Don't let life run away from you. Make sure that you have a good balance of introspection, self-awareness, and action. That's the best way to discover your life purpose.

3. Exercise to begin exploring your life purpose by exploring your curiosity

You might be finding yourself in a curious state of affairs. A few chapters ago, you were just going about your business, but now you suddenly need to get yourself a life purpose. You were happy go lucky until part two of this book. Then I went dark on you and possibly started a full-blown existential crisis where you find yourself without a life purpose in the middle of a dark and cold universe, coming to terms with the personal inadequacies you might have stumbled upon while looking inward.

It's not all bad. I have a cute little exercise to help you as you stare into an existential abyss.

This is an exercise that helped me when I was trying to grow my own self-awareness, and nail down the direction of my own life. I used to go to big bookstores like Borders, Barnes & Noble, or whichever one hasn't been killed by Amazon by the time you are reading this, and browse book topics to see which ideas inspired my curiosity. I used to love browsing philosophy books, classic novels, how-to, and even self-help books. I would open ones that looked good and read a few pages from them. I could spend hours in a bookstore dreaming about which book would give me the most of what I needed at that moment in my life.

This accomplished a few things. First, I was able to gauge my own interest in different books or topics by comparing my own reaction to them as I browsed them. After I would identify what I was most curious about, I would buy a book on that topic, read it, and explore that curiosity. As I consumed these books, new questions and curiosities would arise from my new knowledge, sending me on more exciting quests of exploring new ideas. This was also a very enjoyable experience in itself. Lastly, this was a way to get educated beyond college or high school. In college or high school, students follow one curriculum suited for everyone, but when you explore your own curiosity, you are creating a curriculum that is ideal for you.

For your exercise, go to a bookstore and browse different books for ideas. See what you are curious about. Read a few pages from a few books while you are in the store to see whether you actually like reading them and whether they inspire you. After you find a book you like, buy it, read it (that's right, actually read it), and repeat this exercise again and again, hopefully for the rest of your life, each time with new curiosities. This process has helped me add depth and different perspectives to my own journey, and solidify my vision for where and how I wanted my life to go. It will help you too.

Regularly reading complex books has another benefit. It will boost your ability to focus on one thing longer and more intensely, and you already know how important that is for productivity.

4. What kind of a legacy would you like to leave?

I keep getting into heavier and heavier topics, don't I? Don't worry, I am not going back on my promise to lighten up. This section was planned during the early stages of this book. Plus, this doesn't have to be heavy. This can be positive, dreamy, and hopeful.

Imagine your ideal legacy. What would it be? What would you want people to say about you? Let yourself sit there and dream about it. Allow yourself to get carried away imagining all the amazing things you can accomplish in your life that can become a part of your legacy. In what state would you like to leave the world after you are gone? This is a question you can take with you as daydream material for the next few days, weeks, and long into the future.

Daydreaming is an amazing tool to let your imagination run wild, and let your subconscious wander to where you/it wants to be, in that feel-good place. Chances are that wherever your subconscious takes you is close to one of your ideal life directions and is a great clue to what your life purpose can be.

You can also do a similar exercise. Imagine how you want people to see you on a daily basis and what you want your image to be now and not just your legacy. Together with your eventual legacy, this will help you identify the direction towards which to move your life.

5. How I discovered my own life purpose by following my own curiosity

I hope you are tired not of hearing my stories. If you are, don't blame me. Blame the people who read my previous books and encouraged me to make them more personal by sharing my own experiences. Now that I've shifted the blame away from myself, let's resume.

When I was a college student, I didn't know much about the world other than what I was fed by the TV channels owned by culture-making corporations. All I knew was how to turn myself into a drone by watching sports and MTV during my free time, and of course, stuff my face with food. Sad, right? I was just one of tens of millions of young people ill-prepared for life by my education and society at large.

Luckily, during my first year of college, I came across a wonderful teacher. His name is Dennis Hendrickson. I can say with some degree of certainty that this man changed my life in a big way. As much as one beacon of light can turn away darkness, his humanities class at City College of San Francisco opened my eyes to literature, music, philosophy,

184

and art, as well as the emotional awareness that comes with them.

In the beginning, it was confusing to absorb and make sense of two and a half thousand years of available art, music and philosophy, but over time, it added an enriching new dimension to my life, and especially my inner life. Discovering them spurned endless curiosity, the pursuit of which helped me become more self-aware and also helped me to realize the purpose of my own life.

Curiosity may not seem like much, but it can move you to action if it grows inside you. That's what happened to me. My curiosity towards different life questions kept growing, and once it got big enough, it became a bigger and bigger part of my daily mental wondering until, despite my inherent human laziness, I could no longer ignore it, and had to pursue it.

That pursuit started with reading books, seeking out classes, learning how to play music, and after many other stops along the way, eventually helped me do better in business.

Yes, somehow it led to business. Weird turn, isn't it? It wasn't immediate, but some of my curiosity led me to pursue my own creative ideas. Most people either ignore their creative ideas or stash them away, but I couldn't do that. Don't get me wrong. I am not saying I am smarter or more special than anyone. In fact, in a way, I believe that opposite is true. I couldn't stop myself from pursuing my own ideas. Some people have the discipline to do that, which leaves them more room in their lives to pursue more practical things. But

I simply couldn't. It is possibly out of my own weakness and delusion that my ideas were interesting enough or worthy of pursuit that I ended up allocating time and effort to work on them. Thus, I turned towards action.

Action is something that sets me apart from most people. I strongly recommend that you follow my lead on this. There is almost no realization of what your life purpose should be without action. Experimenting, trying a million and one things, and gaining life experience will help you identify an ideal path in life.

If you stay within your comfort zone, you are staying comfortable, but comfortable is not an ideal place to be. Life is about endless personal growth. That growth comes from struggle. It comes from the risks and challenges you take on, and your journey to overcome those challenges and triumph.

In today's world, you can have a life that is mostly without struggle. Education is as widely available as ever in more forms than ever. With a reasonable effort, more people than ever are able to make a living with a solid if not an amazing job. Most of your loved ones would be sad to see you struggling. Your parents probably struggled so that you wouldn't have to. But the struggle and the process of overcoming challenges is what makes you stronger and more confident in your abilities and your greater potential.

Don't get me wrong. Struggle isn't fun. It is by definition a negative experience. No one wants to voluntarily be struggling. When you are struggling, every day and hour feels like an eternity. I understand it. I've been there before and I'll be there again many times in my life. But your ability to overcome struggle makes you stronger, gives you new skills, and will set you apart from everyone else.

In my business coaching practice I see entrepreneurs struggling all the time. Many people fail because they are incapable of stepping out of their comfort zone, getting dirty, and learning new skills. My advice is to embrace learning and perfecting skills where you are currently weak. This will turn your weaknesses into strengths. Of course, don't lose sight of the strengths you had to begin with. Definitely double down on your natural strengths. But don't be afraid to go outside them and try things in which you aren't comfortable or strong just yet.

Business today requires skills like managing, organizing, creating video, writing, learning to code, doing sales, and much more. No one was born with these skills. They can all be learned. You don't have to learn all of them, but if you are an entrepreneur, most of the time you won't be able to hire people to do all of these tasks for you, and will have to learn many of these skills. Learning will be a struggle, but once you do, you will have given yourself an advantage.

Let your curiosity blossom to a point that it will be impossible for you not to pursue it. That pursuit, as challenging as it may be, is a gift that only you can give yourself. No one else can peek inside your heart to know what curiosities you need to allow to blossom and pursue. It is up to you so take it seriously. Self-awareness and taking action isn't something you can outsource. It is something you have to master.

How does all this become a business? It wouldn't become a business in all cases, but if you are to pursue your curiosity long-term, you will need to find a way to make that pursuit financially self-sustaining. If you want to do yourself a big service, you would not only pursue your life purpose long-term, but also full-time, and with financial resources behind it. To do that, you must figure out how to turn your life purpose into a business.

Reminder, if you want help brainstorming how to turn your passion or curiosity into a business, feel welcome to email me with questions. Small business development and marketing is one of my areas of expertise, and I may be able to point you in the right direction.

6. Story from Dostoevsky

I am showing off by name dropping Dostoevsky, but at least I am name dropping an intellectual writer instead of Kanye West or something similar?

One of Dostoevsky's books, *The Idiot*, has a sub-story the essence of which repeats throughout literature. I'll tell you about Dostoevsky's version because it makes me feel smarter when I use his name in a sentence.

This story goes like this. It is the early 19th century in Europe, and a man has been sentenced to be executed. The story focuses on what goes through the man's mind as the moment of his execution approaches. The man is naturally panicking. He feels hysterical and remorseful about all the things in his life he wanted to do, hasn't done, and now will never get to do. He admonishes himself for being so wasteful with his time, letting so many days pass by without doing more.

The man thinks to himself that if he only had a chance to do things over, he would squeeze every ounce of life from every living second. He wouldn't be wasteful. He would work on and accomplish great things. Sitting there in his cell, waiting for his execution, he felt that he realized his life's folly, and he would correct it if only he had a second chance. His thoughts got more intense as his death sentence approached, escalating to almost a scream inside his soul.

With only a few minutes remaining before this man was to be executed, he got notice that he had been pardoned. He promised himself that from then on, everything in his life would be different.

Do you think his life was different? It wasn't. Shortly after being pardoned, he went back to his old habits and didn't make any real changes. He lived an uneventful life and simply died later on his own.

That's the end of the story. But what's the point of this story? The point is to illustrate the simplicity of human nature. We don't do much with our lives unless we have a feeling of urgency.

We need a feeling of urgency to move us towards action.

To get a feeling of urgency, think about how fleeting life is, and how little time you have to create your legacy. I want you to feel enough urgency to get you to take action rather than be a passive observer of your life. Don't waste any more moments not having direction. Take the bull by the horns, and never look back.

7. Me-me-me vs. doing something that is a bigger cause

At some level, all of us just want to Netflix and chill, travel, eat, be entertained, and have a nice time. But living a life of comfort and indulgence can get boring because it isn't deeply fulfilling.

Boredom will lead to seeking fulfillment and mental stimulation, which will bring you back to the question of what you should do with your life and what your life purpose should be. Luckily, since you will be bored of indulging in things like traveling, eating, and empty entertainment, your potential answer range will be narrowed to things you can do that are more than seeking simple, self-centered pleasures.

Your choices will be things that are outside of yourself. Some of those choices will be bigger causes to which you can devote yourself like global hunger, violence, animal cruelty, sickness, declining health of our planet, and many others.

You might say that you can't solve these problems by yourself, and I'd agree with you. But you can make a small impact. A small impact in something great and fulfilling can be more meaningful that indulging in something that is purely for your own pleasure.

True fulfillment often comes from working on causes that are greater than yourself. Think about what bigger causes are important to you, and which causes can fulfill you long-term. Those causes are good candidates to become a part of your life's work. Working on bigger causes should make up some of your action/theory practice of exploring your life purpose.

8. Exercise to help discover mind purpose

Here is your simple exercise. Take a piece of paper (which I hope you will recycle later), and do a 15 to 30 minute mind dump of all the things you can think of in the world that you would like to see improved.

You can also use a note-taking app to track your ideas. You can use the app when you are out to write new ideas down whenever inspiration hits you.

Collecting a full list of things you would like to see improved will help you identify many good candidates for your life purpose. Once you are happy with the size and scope of this list, order the list by passion, priority and your ability to make an impact. Once you have this list ordered, it should become much more clear which of these you can add to your life's work or life purpose.

CHAPTER 13:
MOTIVATION

1. Intrinsic vs. extrinsic motivation

When starting your business, you must be extremely motivated. Some motivation can come from your passion for your business, but the real motivator, in the beginning, is usually your inability to afford rent or food if your business doesn't work out. But how do you stay motivated long-term, after you are financially secure?

Some people may suggest that you "treat yourself to something nice like dessert or vacation." Those things are fun while they last, but you can't be on vacation or eat dessert (although I am willing to try) all the time. Plus, the boost from those treats is too short-lived. Alternative forms of short-term motivation include coaching sessions, listening to motivational speakers, random good news, music, etc.

Many people get inspired, make big plans, and proceed to do little to nothing after the initial inspiration wanes. The big question is how to make your motivation last. Let's start with two definitions.

Intrinsic motivation - (from the word internal) motivation that comes naturally from inside of you. An example of that is what you want to do when you first wake up or during your idle time.

Extrinsic motivation - (from the word external) motivation that comes from external sources like music, being coached, attending a motivational seminar, or treating yourself to something nice, etc.

Extrinsic motivation is usually short-lived. Though it is helpful when trying to form healthier habits. Motivating yourself in the moment can help you find the will to start doing actions you need that will help you eventually form productive habits. Habits are arguably better than any kind of motivation because they don't require you to be motivated. They are by definition things that you simply do.

Longer lasting motivation comes from inside. And no, you don't have to swallow anything to get motivation to come from inside. To get long-term intrinsic motivation, you must give yourself a purpose. Your life purpose will serve as the great long-term, intrinsic motivator you need to jump out of bed every morning, raring to go.

Because you need to find the key to intrinsic motivation, the previous chapters focused on helping you:

1) Focus on getting you to know yourself better so that you can uncover the right path towards which to set your life.
2) Identify your life purpose.
3) Made the goal of your work to reach your life purpose, and take away many of the things that don't help you

reach your life purpose.

Once you've chosen the right goals, you will be motivated and chomping at the bit to work towards them because that's what truly excites you.

2. Extra ways to stay motivated long-term

New entrepreneurs look at your bills and get the "I need to scramble my way out of this mess any way possible" motivation. But what happens after that source of motivation is no longer there?

Many people find acts of charity and philanthropy to be extremely motivating. Go back to the exercise from the previous chapter where you examined things that you will want to see improved in the world, and identify a number of charities that you can benefit. Some charities can be helped with direct action, but almost all charities can be helped with cash donations. You can identify charities which can be helped with cash donations which are second to your direct life purpose, and make a plan to donate to them. The more successful you are as an entrepreneur, the more you can donate and benefit those charities. That endless pursuit of being able to give and do more can be an extra motivator to aim much bigger in your business and career.

Being inspired to give more to others has helped many people find an extra boost in motivation, and accomplish more in their own work. Giving to charity and hopefully making the world a better place is something that can be an endless project that gives your life boundless meaning and long-term motivation.

3. Motivation exercise one: plan healthy living into your day

I am neither a doctor nor your mother, so I'll keep this brief. When you are not 100% healthy, there is a direct and significant negative impact on your productivity. Not feeling 100% healthy and energetic takes a toll on your ability to focus, concentrate, your mood, and many other things. Having a negative mood will decrease feelings of being motivated.

On the flip side, if you eat healthier, exercise, keep yourself in good general shape and make sure to get enough sleep, you will immediately boost your mood and overall productivity. Adding exercise to your day is also a fantastic way to immediately improve your mood as exercise helps your body release chemicals called endorphins. Endorphins trigger positive feelings in the body.

Living an overall healthy lifestyle will help you be more productive now and for years to come.

4. Motivation exercise two: checklist of additions to your schedule

Do you remember the schedule I shared with you in the time management chapter? I hope you've started planning and keeping a calendar for your days and weeks. In this section we'll add items to your schedule that will help you maintain health and general well-being for the immediate and long-term.

Checklist of health and wellness items to add to your schedule:

- Wake up time, and time you will go to sleep
- Creative non-main-work projects including reading
- Exercise
- Relaxation
- Family and social time
- Meal preparation
- Stretch breaks after sitting too long

If you are thinking to yourself that you don't have time to add all these things to your day because you are already too busy, realize that doing things in this checklist will help you accomplish more during the time you work, and should more than balance out the time you devote to them.

Add these items to your schedule for the next 3-4 weeks to make sure that you begin turning these tasks into healthy habits, and make them a part of your daily routine.

5. Additional reasons for low motivation

Additional causes of decreased motivation are feelings of being stuck in a rut or a bad daily routine. These feelings can result from simple things like sitting in front of a TV for a long time, being around negative people who bring you down or having to go to a job that you don't like. Even bad weather or poor lighting can make you feel sad and unmotivated.

Additional causes of low motivation can be medical or require the skills of a psychologist or a psychiatrist. That is NOT something I can help with in this book. Luckily, many things that can decrease motivation are caused by poor habits that are within your control. To reverse these bad habits, all you have to do is this three-step process:

1) Practice self-awareness and mindfulness to identify the root cause of your decreased motivation.
2) Consciously realize that this habit is causing damage to your life and decide that you want to take action to reverse that habit.
3) Use your knowledge of how to reverse habits to reverse those habits.

If what's causing you to have low motivation is something big in your life like your job or family, it would be irresponsible of me to try to help or suggest that there is a quick fix. Such situations require help that is beyond what this book can offer.

6. Break big tasks into smaller achievable tasks to give yourself a light at the end of the tunnel

Standing at the foot of a mountain you have to climb can be a daunting experience. How in the world are you supposed to climb that thing? If you keep standing there completely discouraged, the low confidence will snowball and build on itself, destroying your morale and motivation. You might even be tempted to turn around and go home.

But what if you had a guide with you who broke down how

each part of the mountain can be conquered? Conquering the big mountain would seem more feasible because instead of having one big mountain to climb, you would have many little achievable steps.

That is how you have to approach big and seemingly insurmountable tasks that seem so difficult that you lose motivation before you start. Breaking big tasks down into many smaller ones that are easily doable will give you the motivation to move forward. Once you start working on those little tasks, a couple of great things happen.

First, the Zeigarnik effect will compel you to finish what you've started. By the quirk of how our brains are wired, your brain will bug and motivate you to keep working on those little tasks after you've started.

Second, as you keep working on little tasks, accomplishing them, gaining confidence, experience, and building momentum, it will naturally be turning into a habit!

Once your work is a habit that you enjoy and get benefit from, there will be no turning back. You will climb parts of the mountain like Tarzan makes his way through the forest by easily swinging from tree branch to tree branch. It's a far cry from sitting at the base of a mountain and fretting about it.

Starting is sometimes half the battle. Simply starting is often enough of a push to help you feel more motivated.

7. List of 10 short-term things you can do to get more motivation TODAY

1) Treat yourself to a dessert.
2) Go for a walk, play sports or go to the gym.
3) Listen to motivational speakers on YouTube.
4) Hire a coach.
5) Buy yourself something nice.
6) Call a positive friend.
7) Think about how great it would be to enjoy the benefits of whatever you need to motivate yourself about. Picture yourself already getting those benefits. It might inspire you to take action sooner rather than later.
8) Keep a daily routine, starting with a set time to wake up and go to sleep.
9) Listen to motivating music.
10) Find a few inspirational quotes, print them, and post them around your work area.

Super bonus tip: think of me raising one eyebrow in my non-intimidating angry look.

8. Little motivational story

People often ask sports coaches about how they motivate their players. A soccer coach once told me after I asked him about how he motivates his players that he doesn't motivate his players. If a player needs extra motivation or pressure that a coach might provide, that player is not sufficiently in-trinsically motivated to be on the team and needs to get back to the drawing board and do some soul searching to find why he or she is not motivated and how to get back to maximum motivation if that is possible for them.

The responsibility of finding motivation is your own, not an external source. Being highly motivated is almost a prerequisite to competing at anything at a high level.

CHAPTER 14:
GOAL SETTING

1. What are goals & difference of goals vs. dreams

A goal is something specific. It is not a wish, which is something that you simply want to happen.

Here is an example of a wish: "I wish I had a better house."

Here is an example of a goal: "I am going to get a better house within two years. It will be in New York, and I'll need $200,000 for the down payment. I will achieve it by cutting current expenses and adding an extra income stream in addition to my current job."

Checklist for what makes a good goal:

- Deadlines
- Specificity
- Get you excited
- Written down
- Achievable
- Help you get to your life purpose
- Cost in time, money and hard work

Most people have wishes rather than goals. A goal has to be put into action sooner rather than later. If there is no action, the goal will never be achieved.

This book has a recurring theme that has me picturing you rolling your eyes since I've repeated it a few times. That theme is setting your life on a carefully chosen path that *you* chose by deeply understanding who you are, and what's best for you. Goal setting is less potent without you first choosing the right greater purpose and direction for your life.

2. S.M.A.R.T goal-setting

S.M.A.R.T goals is a concept from the 1980s which is still popular. It is geared towards corporate goal-setting rather than personal goal-setting, but it is still very relevant for us. S.M.A.R.T stands for:

Specific - clear and well defined goal.

Measurable - completion point is well understood and clear since progress can be tracked and measured.

Agreed upon - if this is a business goal and there are many stakeholders, they should all agree on it.

Realistic - attainable with the resources you have available.

Timely - has a deadline.

3. Goal setting exercise: create a list of your top-10 goals

You may recall your initial and possibly lasting resentment

towards me when I asked you to take a close look at all your tasks and apply the 80/20 rule to them by cutting out 80% of your tasks that didn't get you closer to your goals or had only mediocre potential.

Now we will apply a similar process to your goals.

Take a pen and paper or open a new text file on your computer, and list 10 dreams you have for yourself and the world. Next to those dreams, rephrase each of them into actionable goals that you can work on and achieve. Make them really big life goals. Suspend your self-restraint to think big here.

Just like we did earlier when we applied the 80/20 rule to things on which you should focus, since I'm feeling kind today, I'll let you turn this into a 70/30 rule and ask you to get rid of your 7 least favorite goals, leaving three goals you want most.

Once you have your most awesome goals chosen, go online and find good visual representations of them. Print the visual representations of your goals and put them up around your work area for daily inspiration and reminders of why you are doing all this in the first place. Those visuals will give you constant extrinsic, short-term motivation to keep you going.

You can add additional visuals of your goals wherever you spend time or see many times each day. It could be a background image on your phone's home screen or something in your car or wallet.

4. Business planning the goals and setting them in motion

Make a mini plan for each goal. If your goal is to start a business, business planning is a standard process. The most important parts of a business plan are:

1) Product
2) Promotion
3) Profitability

If you want to do something like buying a car, you can still plan the steps for it.

An example of a small plan would be:

1) Choose the car you want
2) Estimate the total down payment you need and ongoing monthly payments for the car, insurance, gas and maintenance
3) Evaluate your current earnings and estimate when you can save for the car you want
4) Give yourself a deadline for saving the money
5) If there is additional work that needs to be done to achieve this goal, deliberately put it on your schedule to help you get started with it

You can loosely apply S.W.O.T analysis, which is a business planning principle. S.W.O.T stands for strengths, weaknesses, opportunities, and threats. Here is an example of a SWOT analysis for the goal of buying a car.

Strengths: This is #1 priority. I can negotiate the price of the car down. I can put my current car as a down payment.

<u>Weaknesses:</u> Insufficient current monthly salary and too many expenses.

<u>Opportunities:</u> I can decrease my other expenses and get an extra part-time job or try to make extra cash online.

<u>Threats:</u> I would have to significantly alter my lifestyle.

5. Why new year resolutions don't work

For most people, new year resolutions are just wishes. People say "this year I want to lose weight." But this isn't an actionable goal.

An actionable goal is something you can put into action. An actionable goal needs a deadline and markers of achievement. It also needs proper planning to make sure that you stay on top of it and continue doing the tasks you need to accomplish the goal. You can use either the power of habit or extrinsic motivation to get you to regularly work on it.

An example of a weight related goal, rather than a wish, is: "I <u>am going to lose 5 pounds</u> in the <u>next 3 months</u> by <u>eating less junk food and exercising at least 5 times per week</u>."

6. Mistake we all make with our goals

If we don't strongly define our goals and life purpose, we become vulnerable and susceptible to having other people's or other organization's agendas and goals handed to us. When we have a goal that we decide on, and are actively working on, we are busy and in motion. Other people's goals simply bounce off us because we don't have time for them.

We can't get distracted. On the other hand, if we allow ourselves to flounder without goals, that creates space for other people's goals to be pushed onto us to which we might be receptive since we don't have any better goals of our own at that moment.

This can result in big, multi-year life mistakes like choosing the wrong thing to study in college, getting into a career you don't love, or getting into wrong types of relationships.

Don't make that mistake. Proactively set your goals and begin working on them.

7. Mistake two: ego-based mental trap that leads to mistakes when setting goals

It is easy to see other people doing well, earning a good salary, getting a new car or house, getting a new iPhone, or just being praised. Seeing these things can make us feel inadequate if we don't already have those things in our lives, and can make us desire those things too. The most ironic thing is that people who show off their possessions or accomplishments the most are people who usually over promote themselves, and don't have it as good as they make it out to be. But we are susceptible to want what they have as soon as we see them having it, and send ourselves on a wild goose chase after what they have, even if that isn't in our goals and isn't going to get us closer to our life purpose.

Simply being aware of the possibility of this happening will help you avoid this mental trap and stay focused on your set goals.

CHAPTER 15:
PROCRASTINATION

1. Procrastination is a habit

Procrastination is a learned behavior and a habit. If you suffer from procrastination, giving you a hard time about it is the best way to start this section because unless your reason for procrastination is clinical, you already have all the tools to reverse your procrastination habit, so please begin taking deliberate action to do so.

The second part of this book has been a journey to give you the tools you need to:

- Be more self-aware
- Discover what you are meant to do in life
- Get incredible motivation from finding fulfilling work
- Get organized, schedule the right things and take out all the things detracting from your work and life
- Set goals and begin working on them

I wrote this book with this structure because one of the challenges most entrepreneurs face that leads to failure is simply not doing enough work. With the tools in this book, you can now overcome this hurdle.

The challenge I have for you is to practice self-awareness and mindfulness, and honestly answer to yourself whether you have been too easy on yourself and let your procrastination problem linger and worsen. I don't need the answer to that question. This is the level of honesty you owe to yourself. If you suffer from procrastination, you have to unearth the reason for your procrastination problem, and take deliberate steps to make necessary changes.

In this chapter, we'll take a closer look at common reasons people procrastinate. And you guessed it, I'll give you some habit building exercises which you won't do. Wait, you will do them, right? Yes? Good.

As we go through this chapter, keep in mind that procrastination is a habit. It is a learned behavior that is in your power to change by building other, healthier habits to counteract the damaging behavior. It can be that easy. Change is a small step away.

2. Procrastination before sitting down to do a task

How can you boost your productivity by using the tips in the other chapters of this book if you don't even sit down to work in the first place? Let's tackle this issue first.

Failure to start is a common problem for students who procrastinate with homework and for entrepreneurs who turn themselves into dreamers and not doers.

Here are some common reasons people fail to start:

1) Competing priorities
2) Uncomfortable workareas
3) External distractions
4) Overwhelming and daunting tasks
5) You suck

Number 5 was a joke. I hope you don't mind me having a little fun here.

Some of these reasons are easily fixable. If the work is low priority for you, you just have to reassess your tasks and reconsider your priorities by being honest with yourself. We've been over that. If you get distracted by TV or people chatting with you on your phone, you have to put away the remote and your phone. If the work feels daunting, "undaunt" it (yes I just made that word) by breaking it into smaller and more manageable tasks. If your work area is not comfortable, clean, organize, or remodel it to be more conducive to producing good work. You can take the remodeling idea one step further by reconfiguring your whole living space to make it easier to get to your work area and more inconvenient to access entertainment like your TV, which is a productivity killer and a common cause of procrastination.

Many people don't own a TV because it is a great cause of procrastination. If you can get rid of your TV, you will immediately save time and money by not having a TV, cable, Netflix, or all the other entertainment services. If you own a TV, you probably lose at least a few hours a week of potentially productive time watching it. Imagine how much you can accomplish with your life and business if you didn't own a TV.

3. Are you avoiding unpleasant tasks? Make them more tolerable

Many people procrastinate because their task at hand seems either difficult, boring, or otherwise unpleasant.

Can you guess how I'll suggest making your task more pleasant? It isn't too different than other strategies we used to solve productivity problems in other chapters. You have to break the big task that is causing you to procrastinate into many smaller and more manageable tasks.

4. Have you turned yourself into a dreamer and not a doer?

Out of any other section in this book, this one is where I have to play detective the most. Dreamers rarely admit that they are dreamers. They vigorously argue that they are doers and that despite not doing much in the past, they will change and begin to take action right away. Even when challenged and asked why they have done so much talking and so little doing, their answer usually glosses over why they have flaked on themselves and typically includes the lie that starting from now on everything will be different.

Of course, nothing changes the next day and they do just as little as before. It becomes impossible to believe people's reasons why they keep procrastinating.

I am neither a psychologist nor a detective, but if I had to guess, I'd say that there are two reasons why this happens:

1) Self deception and delusion

2) Simple attention seeking

If this is something that happens to you, believe it or not, you and I are in the same boat in that we are both scratching our heads, wondering how to get you to do more. After all, I am here to help you succeed, and I spend a lot of time thinking about how to help people in this situation.

If this is something that happens to you, based on my work with clients suffering from a similar issue, my guess is that you are simply pursuing the wrong project that is a mismatch for your abilities or true priorities.

For example, your business might require a lot of money or skills you don't have, more effort than you are able to give, or anything else overwhelming and seemingly insurmountable. The project you chose may be bumping up against too many of your weaknesses. We all have weaknesses. The key is to choose a strategy that is least inhibited by your weaknesses, and takes the biggest advantage of your natural strengths.

Even if you are brilliant in what you do best, when it comes to working on your current task, you may not be putting yourself in a position to apply your best skills. You might even realize that this is the case, but it might simply be too difficult to change course because you've invested so much time and effort into your current path.

Instead of digging yourself further into this fruitless hole, it might be more prudent to rethink your strategy and choose one that emphasizes your talents instead of your weaknesses.

People who are aware of this issue and have not made the appropriate changes usually feel frozen because the changes require a big and scary life shift. Such a life shift might require you to give up something that you have invested emotion and money into, but by not making a choice and doubling down on your lost cause, you are making your procrastination and related problems worse on a daily basis.

I don't want to tell you what to do when it comes to making big and challenging life decisions, but let me tell you what to do. Just kidding. Maybe I am not kidding all that much. As I see it, you have three ways to go:

1) Get help to make yourself better at what you are trying to do through education, coaching, mentoring, or by joining a peer support or mastermind group.
2) Switch your strategy so that your work takes advantage of your strengths and incorporates things that make you happier. Yeah, I know. This is easier said than done.
3) Keep doing the same thing you've been doing and continue wasting your own, and everyone else's, time.

Luckily there is a fourth option. You can suspend your current project, the one you are procrastinating on anyway, and focus on getting more money or on getting your life on track. Once you find yourself in a more financially stable situation, you can put money towards hiring extra help, coaching or outsourcing. If you make yourself more financially solvent when you get back to your project, you will be able to give it a bigger, better and more concentrated effort that will have a stronger strategy and a better chance to succeed.

5. Is perfectionism preventing you from starting?

If your problem is perfectionism, I must admit that I don't quite understand you. I have the exact opposite problem - I launch too early rather than waiting until something is perfect.

But while thinking of a witty opening for this section, I experienced procrastination due to perfectionism. I wanted to come up with something truly witty to open this section.

As you see (more like didn't see) there was nothing too witty to start this section. I went with the imperfect opening, and left the pursuit of the perfect joke for later.

Follow my lead and understand that in almost all cases, you can improve what you create even after you've launched.

In school, our projects have deadlines and we get immediate grades on our projects. In life, this dynamic is slightly different. In life, we are often given the opportunity to keep improving our skills and what we create. Even if you might get a D- in life, you can keep improving what you made until it is a C, B and eventually an A+.

The key is to get started and take the initial pressure off yourself. Find a way to give yourself that initial push, possibly with short-term extrinsic motivation. Once you get started, it might put you on a roll and give you creative momentum. Before you know it, you will be done with your task like I am with this section.

How do you like that for "show, don't tell?"

6. Do you work better under pressure

I once had a client who told me that he worked better under pressure. I offered to come over and threaten violence to make him feel pressure. He declined. I then offered to raise my rate if he continued to procrastinate. He agreed to that. I thought it would help, but he still procrastinated. After that, we created shorter deadlines for him for which he was supposed to have smaller and more manageable deliverables. That also didn't work. After that, I experimented with staying with him while he worked. That worked, but it was impossible for me to stay with him throughout all his work. As soon as I left, he reverted back to procrastinating.

If this sounds like your experience, find business partners, work partners, accountability partners, or buddies who will keep you on track.

7. Fear of criticism

Fear of criticism is sometimes related to procrastination due to perfectionism with one twist. That twist is a projection of negativity which results in fear of public embarrassment.

One way to fix this is for yourself to become more positive and optimistic. I realize that is easier said than done, but if you can manage it, that positivity will make you project and expect more positive reactions and outcomes, and help you get over procrastination that is due to a fear of criticism.

Common ways to immediately feel more positive is to get some exercise, good sleep, eat better, and do many of the additional health-boosting activities we've already covered.

214

8. Distractions causing procrastination?

Many people procrastinate because after sitting down to work, they get distracted from what they need to be doing with alerts from their phone, Facebook, news, friend messages, email, and other distractions.

Luckily, we went over tools, apps and techniques to get rid of those distractions and interruptions earlier in this book. If you suffer from procrastination rooted in distraction, go back over the techniques to boost your focus and minimize interruptions, and work on incorporating them in your daily work habits.

9. Adding accountability: having deadlines imposed on you

Holding yourself accountable to complete your tasks will help you overcome procrastination. Luckily, if you have correctly set goals for yourself, those goals have a deadline on them which gives you naturally built in accountability. Since many people like to work with tight deadlines, that alone should help you decrease procrastination. If it isn't enough, here are a few more tactics to increase accountability:

- Post your current task on Facebook or other social media websites. Just having other people see it will make you feel a little bit embarrassed if you don't work on it, and might give you the push you need to get started.
- Get a family member or a friend to check up on you.
- If you are starting a business, a co-founder is the ideal person to work next to you and keep you on track.
- Hire someone like a coach to help stay on top of your

work and make sure you do what you have to.

Here is a business idea that occurred to me while writing this section - an online or local community of accountability buddies who keep each other on track? This would help people who procrastinate, and members would pay you to join the group and remain members. All readers of this book are welcome to steal this business idea.

10. Checklist of quick procrastination wins you can do now

- Empty your work area of clutter and make it a nice, clean, and pleasant environment
- Turn off your TV
- Put your phone away or turn it off
- Use software to block websites which distract you from your work
- Let more natural sunlight into your work area
- Go to a quiet place to work
- Hire a coach to help you

11. Experiment to try with TV and Facebook

If by reading the title of this section you got excited about an experiment that will involve you watching TV while surfing Facebook, I am sorry because the experiment is to NOT watch TV or log onto Facebook. If TV or Facebook are not your vices, be honest and replace TV and Facebook with your vices.

The experiment is to quit your vice for two days, cold turkey.

Just don't turn on your TV and don't log onto Facebook. If you avoid the vices that cause you to procrastinate, my hope is that it will open up space in your life to make you so bored that you will be forced to start on the task that you need to be working on.

Once you begin work on your task, this should help you realize the extent of the damage that your vice is doing to your life. If you see enough damage to your life from your vice, and how much work you can be accomplishing if you get rid of it, my hope is that it will make you take a pause and say to yourself "hmmm, that TV is really killing my productivity much more than I thought. That is a problem. I should fix this issue."

Once you identify the problem and see the extent of its damage on your life, you will be more inclined to take action towards fixing it. Luckily, by now you know how to reverse problematic habits and replace them with healthier ones.

12. Rewarding yourself

I usually don't love reward-based motivation because if the reward is a snack, extra TV time, or something else that is relatively simple, you can easily cheat and treat yourself to the reward even if you fail to do the work to earn the reward. Who are we kidding with this reward thing?

But isn't the real reward your greater goal? That is an infinitely more powerful and compelling reward than a cheap short-term thrill.

If you are procrastinating because you feel that you need a

push, keep picturing and dreaming about your greater goals. If your goal is an incredible reward, it will motivate you and help you break your procrastination cycle.

13. Procrastinating vs. prioritizing

Are you ready for a moment of irony?

Identify the task you are procrastinating on and your main distraction from it. Which one of the two is more important for you? You might be telling yourself that the task you are procrastinating on is more important, but by allowing yourself to be distracted from it, you are prioritizing whatever you are allowing the distraction to be. Your subconscious is prioritizing the distraction. Think about it. This might be a clue to what's truly more important for you, and you may be deceiving yourself on a subconscious level.

14. Chapter conclusion

Since there are many reasons why people procrastinate, without having a conversation with you about it, I can't tell you which reason is causing you to procrastinate.

What I can do for you is to offer extra help that goes beyond this book. You are welcome to email me and we can discuss your current challenges and how to get past them. Here is my personal email:

alex.genadinik@gmail.com

Just keep in mind that I am often overwhelmed with the amount of email that I get. If you can keep your initial email brief and specific, it would make it much easier for me to respond quickly.

And of course, if your email starts with something like "I really love your book, and I left a glowing review about it on Amazon." you will immediately become one of my favorites and I'll do my best to answer ASAP.

If I don't hear from you, just practice self-awareness by listening to your inner voice, and by identifying the emotions and thought process that cause you to procrastinate.

You don't have to perfectly identify it on your first try, but if you feel that you suffer from procrastination, you would be well advised to keep digging deeper within yourself in order to identify the root of your procrastination so that you can begin to reverse the root cause.

CHAPTER 16:
MEETING PRODUCTIVITY

I saved meeting productivity for last because it offers a good reminder of the common meeting productivity principles like focus, goal-setting, and taking leadership and responsibility for your own success and productivity. This chapter will serve as a great recap of other productivity principles we discovered throughout this book.

1. Meeting facilitator

Just like your personal productivity journey starts with you wanting to be more productive and taking on the leadership role in choosing the direction of your life, meetings need leadership too. A meeting leader is usually called a facilitator. The facilitator is typically the one who organizes the meeting, invites participants, schedules it, reserves meeting space, creates the meeting agenda and facilitates the meeting when it occurs.

The facilitator has another important job which is to keep everyone focused on accomplishing the meeting's goals. Every once in a while, you will have a "meeting hijacker" which is a person who takes the meeting in a direction that isn't the meeting's main focus. Just like you must police yourself to keep your own long-term and immediate focus crystal clear, it is the job of the meeting facilitator to police the meeting to always bring it back on topic if the meeting gets hijacked.

2. Meeting goal

Just like you need to set goals in your life, every meeting must have stated goals that are stated when you set up the meeting and invite people to it. The meeting goals should also be repeated at the beginning to help get all the participants on the same page.

3. Meeting duration and deadline

Every meeting should have a stated duration. A set time frame helps everyone focus on accomplishing the goals of the meeting and minimizes small talk and other side topics.

4. Seating arrangements

If you are having a brainstorming or a team-building meeting, it is helpful for everyone to face each other by sitting in a circle or a rectangle.

If you have negotiations during the meeting, the seating arrangement should be arranged in your favor by tapping into the subconscious. Dress your sharpest and look your most professional. Choose the best and highest chair. Many firms have specific meeting rooms where on one side of the table the chairs are a little higher and on the other, the chairs are a little lower and less comfortable. During negotiations, the host company chooses the better and higher chairs, and leaves the smaller chairs to the visiting team. Subconsciously, that gives the hosts more confidence and a small advantage.

THE END

Thank you for reading. I appreciate that you made it here. While the book is over, our journey isn't.

Here is what to do next:

1) Keep reading to learn about all the free extra resources and gifts you get.

2) Reach out to me any time with questions.

3) Practice your new productivity principles.

FURTHER FREE RESOURCES AND DISCOUNTS

Gift 1: One free online business or marketing course of YOUR choosing.

I teach over 100 online courses on business and marketing topics. For being a reader of this book, I will give you one course absolutely free. You get to choose which one. Browse my full list of courses, email me telling me which course you want, and I will send you a free coupon!

Here is my full list of courses:

https://www.udemy.com/user/alexgenadinik/

Just send me an email to alex.genadinik@gmail.com and tell me that you got this book, and which of my courses you would like for free.

Gift: 2: Get my iPhone and Android business apps for free.

My apps come as a 4-app series on iPhone and Android. I have free versions of each app!

The links here are shortened to help you type them into your browser if you got the print version of the book and can't simply click the link like you could if you had the Kindle version of the book.

Free Android business plan app:

https://goo.gl/GDl0TB

Free Android marketing app:

https://goo.gl/jhsWt6

Free Android app on fundraising and making money:

https://goo.gl/BcAX60

Free business idea Android app:

https://goo.gl/niEjaH

Free business idea iPhone app:

https://goo.gl/eyKEzT

Free iPhone business plan app:

https://goo.gl/VBWtsC

Free iPhone marketing app:

https://goo.gl/8Il12P

Free iPhone app for fundraising:

https://goo.gl/WO1L53

Gift 3: Free business advice

If you have questions about your personal productivity challenges, your overall business, or anything mentioned in this book, email me at alex.genadinik@gmail.com and I will be happy to help you. Just please keep two things in mind:

1) Remind me that you got this book and that you are not just a random person on the Internet.
2) Please make the questions clear and short. I love to help, but I am often overwhelmed with work and email, and always short on the time. The more clear you are in your questions, the more clear I can be in my response.

Gift 4: More free products

When I have free promotions for my products, the four places where I post them are my YouTube channel, my email list, Twitter, and my Facebook group. If you subscribe, you will get my future updates about free products. Just keep in mind that I promote everything and anything business related on my social media accounts so it won't just be the freebies.

Sign up for my email list:

http://glowingstart.com/email-subscribe/

YouTube channel where you can subscribe:

http://www.youtube.com/user/Okudjavavich

Facebook group you can join:

https://www.facebook.com/groups/problemio/

You can also follow me on Twitter @genadinik

COMPLETE LIST OF MY BOOKS

If you enjoyed this book, check out my Amazon author page to see the full list of my books. Here is a shortened URL that will redirect to the page with all my books on Amazon:

https://goo.gl/CA5Tzn

All my books can also be found on my website:

http://www.problemio.com

DID YOU ENJOY THE BOOK?

If you liked the book, I would sincerely appreciate it if you left a review about your experience on Amazon.

If you didn't enjoy it, or were expecting to get different things out of it, please email me at alex.genadinik@gmail.com and I will be happy to add or edit material in this book to make it better.

Thank you for reading and please keep in touch!

ABOUT THE AUTHOR

Alex Genadinik is a software engineer, an entrepreneur, and a marketer. Alex is a 3-time best selling Amazon author, and the creator of the Problemio.com business apps which are some of the top mobile apps for planning and starting a business with 1,000,000 downloads across iOS, Android and Kindle.

Alex has a B.S in Computer Science from San Jose State University.

Alex is also a prominent online teacher, and loves to help entrepreneurs achieve their dreams.

Printed in Great Britain
by Amazon